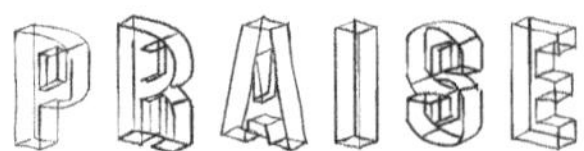

PRAISE

In *Math Play*, Libo takes his readers through his journey as a teacher and parent on a quest to make math joyful for every learner. He pairs strategies and lesson plans with research and interviews and weaves in anecdotes from his classroom and from engaging in MathPlay with his young daughter throughout. *Math Play* is a fantastic read for not only math teachers but also for parents, particularly those with young children. Libo's passion and generosity leap from the page in this book. *Math Play* is such an enjoyable read, packed with practical ideas, photo visuals, and detailed lessons that you'll be able to use right away.

Stacey Roshan
Educator | Edtech Consultant | Author

Mathematics is a fundamentally human enterprise that has engaged humankind for thousands of years. And what exactly has engaged humans so? Surely not success on standardized tests, the completion of worksheets, and other "pushups" for demonstrating procedural fluency. No, the goal for engaging in mathematics is to experience and master the awe, power, and profound agency mathematics can bring. Libo Valencia beautifully shares with us personal context, story, and his favorite resources for bringing true human engagement with mathematics to one and all.

James Tanton
The Global Math Project

For those interested in making math more joyful and meaningful, Libo Valencia invites you into his vibrant classroom. This book will jump-start your *Math Play* journey with its detailed examples and suggestions.

Berkeley Everett
Math Coach & Consultant

Libo understands to his core that play is the great under-utilized ingredient for creating meaningful math learning experiences. His delightful stories of MathPlay with his daughter and students show just how wonderful this subject can be when we begin with play. The fact that he takes a tour of some of the best resources math educators have produced in the last decade will make this book useful to readers ready to start their MathPlay journey!

Dan Finkel
Founder, Math for Love

Oftentimes, the subject area of mathematics comes with negative connotations. *Math Play* helps the reader break through this barrier with a fresh approach that taps into the playfulness and curiosity of educators and students! Libo makes a strong case that we can leverage math, across all ages, to help students to continue to embrace their childlike wonder while at the same time learning grade level content. As a practitioner, the author draws upon many examples from his current classroom and educators reading this book will feel confident they can implement MathPlay with their very own students! Highly recommended.

Ross Cooper
Assistant Principal | Author

Libo Valencia has written a playful and engaging book on the integration of mathematics and play. As mathematics teachers and leaders, we have to ensure our classrooms are joyful for all students to learn and this book provides a window on how to do that well! Libo shows real world examples both from his classroom and from his own life at home that help to shine a light on how rigorous mathematics standards and play intersect. This is a must have book for all readers who want to bring more joy into the mathematics classroom while also engaging students in mathematical reasoning, discourse, and thinking!

Georgina Rivera
NCSM Vice President | Principal

Math Play

First edition 2023

For Carolina, Mariana, and Madeline

LIBO VALENCIA

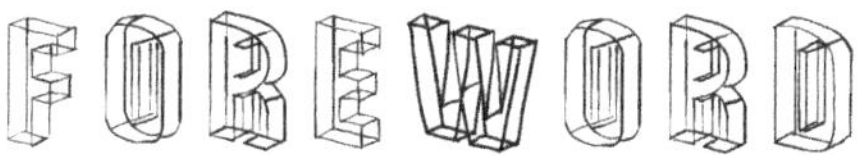

FOREWORD

BRIAN ASPINALL

"All we do is play in Mr. Aspinall's class," my students would say as they planned their eighth grade graduation parties. For over a decade I would cower in the corner of my classroom as I listened to my graduating class reflect on their tenth and final year of elementary school.

"I wish he had prepared me more for high school," other students would say.

While we spend the majority of our time as educators providing students with feedback, it can be challenging for us to accept criticism from those same learners—the ones we teach and the ones who teach us. In this case, my students had already decided what high school looked like before their arrival. Word on the street was that our local high school spent a great deal of time focusing on note taking, rote memorization, and test taking. While these skills are important, I have yet to find a curriculum document that outlines note taking as a skill I should be evaluating. When we focus our energies on the clerical idea of how information is delivered from educator to student, we reduce the exploration of why we have chosen to teach using these such methods.

"Because that is how we have always done it."

I've heard this statement countless times in different school staff rooms. This idea feels comforting from an efficiency standpoint, suggesting the workload to complete the mission is formulaic as it has been proven year after year. However, students who began high school in 2019 will certainly finish it much differently this calendar year. There is no more formula for routine. The only constant we need is change and when we become comfortable with discomfort, real innovation can begin.

In my first few years as an elementary school teacher, I would attempt to dissect what exactly was meant by *preparation for high school.* After all, hadn't we spent the last ten years of elementary school preparing students for their open next steps?

Being a middle school teacher proved to be challenging. I was responsible for those grades between standardized testing years. In the province of Ontario our students write standardized tests in third, sixth and ninth grade. I always enjoyed teaching the years in between. It was as if we were free to explore and not be tied to the paradox of standardized testing.

Why do we spend the bulk of our teaching trying to solidify the narrative that we learn from reflecting on mistakes, taking risks, and trying new things, only to put students in isolated rows, remove the year's worth of scaffolds, and evaluate student progress based on the results on one isolated test? This same test communicates to students that mistakes are bad, perfection is crucial, and performing well signifies achieving a quantity of correct answers in a specified amount of time.

As Libo says, "Learning takes time and making mistakes is part of that journey."

Math Play is a beautiful synergy of passion, reflection, work, and play. Consider for a second *work* and *play* as synonymous. It would appear that as we climb through the grades of just about every K-12 education system, a wedge is driven between the concept of work and play suggesting that the older we get the less important play is and what really counts is our ability to complete work.

I first met Libo online when his math tweets caught my attention. I was ridiculously excited to find a high school math educator focusing more on play, less on work (in the traditional sense), and really trying to showcase the value of learning over grades. What makes Libo's story incredibly special is how he articulates the intersection of play and work, thus blurring the lines between isolated definitions.

As an educator for the last seventeen years, I have come to learn that the purpose of school if you will, has changed significantly. Once upon a time I recall being told to get good grades in order to get a good job.

Does this matter of fact opinion still hold true today? Did it ever? How has the work industry changed in the last few decades? Has education done the same?

I love sharing the stories of Steve Jobs, AirBnB, and Uber during my keynote addresses. I feel incredibly lucky to be able to travel across the globe to consult and work with school, union, and government teams in the education space. A common theme among these groups is the narrative of problem solving, critical thinking, collaboration, and currently, coding and artificial intelligence. I often wonder why we preach these key ingredients as mandatory for success but also close out each and every school year by passing out report cards which show students what they scored in each class. For the most part, that score is determined by a quantity of correct answers. This counterproductive thinking is not only confusing to kids, but to us as educators. I have yet to meet a teacher who didn't want what was best for all students, while trying to navigate the misleading initiatives set out by people above us on the internal, corporate ladder.

Steve Jobs, more specifically, the success of iDevices, stems from the results of solving a very simple problem. At the turn of the century, we saw headlines about a massive band known as Metallica, hammering down on a handful of teenagers for sharing their music on a program they coded themselves. Napster was game changing for the entertainment industry and led to an incredible disruption. In order to alleviate the concerns over music piracy, Jobs decided iTunes was the solution. Now people could purchase singles as well as full length albums, thus reducing the trading of hit songs. But it didn't end there. The real innovation came in the form of said devices, the only means to listen to this new music service.

My love for AirBnB and Uber derives from the notion that these two businesses, two of the most successful in the world, do not directly sell their own products or services. Instead, they empower members of their community to strive for success within the parameters set by the apps themselves. Imagine if our classrooms operated in the same manner.

What if our classrooms focused more on individual accomplishments than an overall school wide score? I anticipate many readers to pushback this idea suggesting that classrooms do, in fact, focus on the individual student. However, at some point, a school, family of schools, or even district leaders have to make decisions based solely on large data sets, not individual scores. While this is important for systemic change and growth, we need a mindset of generalized district initiatives when dissecting the needs of our individual students. What works for some may not work for all. AirBnB and Uber conduct themselves similarly. They do not dictate the types of vehicles to drive or the best time of day to do so. They do not mandate a set number of bedrooms per rental or suggest certain shower stalls will make every single guest happy. Instead, they offer support, research, ideas, and suggestions for success but ultimately leave it to each individual to determine their best approach. While our older students are more capable of such independence, it is our youngest learners who are most interested in soaking up the learning provided to them.

Math Play tells the story of a phenomenal high school math educator on a mission to disrupt math classrooms across the globe by focusing our attention on learning first and grades second. When we let evaluation dictate our lessons, we are often left with quizzes and worksheets because they are the quickest way to evaluate and provide concrete evidence of where students are. I use the term *evidence* loosely because we do not judge Sydney Crosby's ability to play hockey by the results of one period, one game, or even one season. And if he does perform poorly, we try to determine why, rather than punish the result or label it as failure.

Libo remarkably explores what learning looks like with his daughters and makes the comparison to his own classrooms through the assessment and evaluation lens. While the scaffolding, ideas, teachings, lessons, and explorations with his young daughters mimic those of his teenage students, the real value lies in what we understand about the learning in Libo's own home. He describes in great detail the love of learning his oldest daughter demonstrates, her thirst for understanding why certain answers are what they are, and her inquisitive approach to understanding her world more by exploring patterns, numbers, data, and manipulatives.

It doesn't take a rocket scientist to discover and understand why Libo's daughters are curious learners. While Libo instructs his lessons at school and home similarly, his daughters are fully aware that they have the freedom to make mistakes, explore, tinker, and ask questions and that they do not have an exam to write at the end of the term. His daughters also have yet to separate the notion of work and play when it comes to mathematics because the system barriers of assessment and evaluation (data, report cards, compliance, etc.) do not exist.

I encourage you, regardless of the subject area you teach, to be critical of your own practice as you explore MathPlay. The best we can do for all of our students is a personal deep dive on our own educational pedagogy.

ACKNOWLEDGMENTS

First and foremost, I want to thank my family. Mariana and Madeline, you are the true inspiration behind *MathPlay*. Your curiosity, love for learning, and willingness to play with dad made MathPlay possible. Always remember that we love you and there is no limit to what you girls can accomplish with hard work and dedication. Carolina, you have taught me that sometimes things go better than we planned. Forming a family together has been the greatest gift of my life; your love, support, and advice have helped me become the "Tata" I'm today. Te Amo!

To my dad, thank you for teaching me the true value of education and for always believing in me. To my mom, thank you for teaching me what character looks like in the face of adversity. Viviana, thank you for sharing your joy with all of us, for as long as I can remember you have always made me smile sis. Titi, thank you for being the rock we can all rely on. I love you all.

To the Code Breaker team, thank you Brian Aspinall, for giving me the opportunity and platform to share my MathPlay story. Thank you for valuing and amplifying teacher voices. Thank you to Daphne McMenemy for helping me find clearer ways to share my thinking, for broadening my perspective, and for bringing *Math Play* to life. I appreciate how you guided me through this process and I feel so fortunate to have collaborated with you.

I would also like to express my gratitude to the school communities where I have worked. White Plains High School is where I started my teaching career and met two lifelong mentors. Lisa Weber, thank you for believing in me from day one. Albert Laporte, your timely advice and support have been so impactful, thank you. At New Rochelle High School, thank you Ronald Morris for giving me a new class every year you were my supervisor, I learned so much from you. At Lehman College, thank you Nicholas Hanges, who is no longer with us, for teaching me PDE while we analyzed possible World Cup match results.

Thank you to the administrators, teachers, students, and families of my current home, the Chappaqua Central School District. Also, special thanks to Tony Sinanis for encouraging me to share my MathPlay message from the beginning.

To all the educators on Twitter who have supported and shared MathPlay ideas, thank you! Let's continue to spread the joy of mathematics for all.

Finally, thank you to every student I had the opportunity and privilege to teach in the past fourteen years. You have inspired me to work hard to become a better teacher every year.

TABLE OF CONTENTS

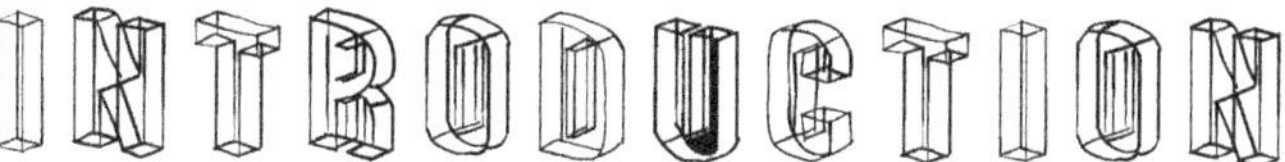

INTRODUCTION

NOBODY CARES HOW MUCH YOU KNOW,
UNTIL THEY KNOW HOW MUCH YOU CARE.

THEODORE ROOSEVELT

MY MATH STORY

GROWING UP IN COLOMBIA, I knew I wanted to work in a math related field one day. As a student, I did very well in all my classes, but I always felt like a fish in water whenever I was in math class. Numbers made sense to me from very early on. I was always amazed by the consistency one can find in mathematics and this turned into a lifelong special connection. In school, whenever I was helping a classmate with math it all felt very natural. As a kid, I felt that math was sort of my superpower.

Let's fast forward to the present. I have been teaching math at the high school and college levels for the past fourteen years. I have worked at different school districts (White Plains, New Rochelle, and Chappaqua) and colleges (Lehman, Manhattanville, and Mercy) all within New York State. Occasionally, during normal interactions, I get to share what I do for a living. This can happen during small talk at the grocery store or during a visit to the doctor. The reaction however, is typically along the same lines: I'm not a math person, I hate math, why do we learn math? or I never use what I learned in math class. If you're a math educator, I bet you probably have found yourself in similar situations. As someone who is passionate about mathematics and teaching it, it's hard to hear such negative reactions towards something I deeply love and enjoy.

Usually, the conversation transitions into me trying to justify the original math complaint. It kind of feels like I'm doing a short and casual math therapy session. I believe that these negative feelings of phobia and anxiety towards math start to develop very early at the elementary levels. I also feel that parents and teachers sometimes inadvertently pass their own feelings towards math to their children or students. I don't think math itself is the problem. I think Larry Martinek really captured this idea when he said, "Children don't hate math. What they hate is being confused, intimidated, and embarrassed by math. With understanding comes passion, and with passion comes growth–a treasure is unlocked." Maybe the way we teach math triggers these negative feelings in some of our learners developing the idea that not liking math is not only socially acceptable but to some degree the expectation.

As many other math educators worldwide, I don't believe there are "math people" and "non-math people." I believe we are all math people. However, my experience as an educator has taught me two very important lessons. First, many people confuse the ability to perform rapid computations with being good at math. Second, many people believe there is a unique way to solve math questions and you either get it or you don't. These two ideas present a very limited view of mathematics and how we learn it. Sadly, these two ideas combined can have a very powerful or devastating impact in how people feel about math. The truth is that taking your time to understand math concepts does not make you bad at math (if you don't believe me, look up Laurent-Moise Schwartz) and more often than not there are multiple ways to approach math questions.

I strongly believe that math is a universal subject that we should all be enjoying. Why do I think it is universal? When I moved to the United States, I did not speak a word of English but was enrolled in an English speaking math class with Mrs. Weber at White Plains High School in New York. I did not understand what was being said in class, but I understood the math. There is definitely something very special about mathematics. Being a teenager in a new country while trying to adjust was definitely challenging, but once again, I felt like I was home in math class. This was an amazing experience that speaks to the beauty of math and that's precisely when I knew I was going to become a math educator.

Early in my teaching career, one of my main goals was to have my students fall in love with math. I wanted all my students to appreciate the beauty of mathematics and to enjoy it as much as I did. As you may already know or have experienced yourself, math is not the most popular of subjects in schools and I believe we can change this! I learned that many high school students come into our classrooms with a pretty well-defined "math identity" they believe to be true and fixed. This is something I have noticed at the various school districts and colleges I have taught at. It's also worth mentioning I have taught different levels: essential, standard, and advanced.

The first years in the teaching profession can be very overwhelming. According to the US Department of Education, nearly 50% of new teachers leave the profession within their first five years. Looking back, I feel my first years as a teacher were very positive. I was writing lesson plans and following all the required guidelines I needed to follow, however, I did not feel like that was enough to engage all my students the way I wanted. As someone who is passionate about math, I felt that if my students could see the power of mathematics in real-life examples, it would contribute to higher levels of engagement and to help change the negative perception of math class. I have always felt very comfortable using technology and as a result I have been eager and open to try new technologies that I thought could be beneficial for my students and their levels of engagement. In my experience, using application examples in my lessons and different technologies in the classroom has been beneficial to engage my students but not always enough.

Very often our students learn mathematics within a predetermined path with very little or no room for exploration and discovery. In full disclosure, I have experienced such lessons myself both as a student and an educator. This idea of a predetermined path reminds me of race horses wearing blinders, which are intended to avoid any distractions due to their peripheral vision. Our math confidence gets built over time. As a math student, I was successful in following my teacher's predetermined path which gave me the confidence to be resilient whenever I experienced difficulty. However, having all students follow the same predetermined pathway may not always be the best option.

As an educator, I try to present different ways to solve questions whenever possible. In my experience, showing multiple approaches can be extremely beneficial for all students. I learned that using multiple paths can help students make connections across different topics and it can also help students develop a deeper understanding of the mathematics they are learning. I believe those are some of the immediate benefits of using multiple approaches. In the long run, using multiple paths discourages the idea that there is a unique or predetermined way to learn mathematics.

So, what is the most effective way to engage students in math class? Is it by implementing the latest technology in the classroom? Embedding real application problems into our lessons? Is it by exploring different approaches with our students? Or is it something else entirely? I'm sure we have all experienced different strategies that work best for us and our learners. These are just a few examples that I've found to be very effective, but once again, not always enough.

After fourteen years of working as an educator, I wholeheartedly believe that the best way any teacher can engage students is by connecting with them beyond the content they teach. Think of your favorite class or teacher when you were in school. Was there a connection beyond the content you were learning? This book is about MathPlay, a very effective and useful strategy to engage students in math class and beyond. Nevertheless, the effectiveness of any strategy you implement in the classroom depends on how well you are able to connect with your students. Your students need to know that you care about them more than you care about what you teach. If your students know how much you care about them, they will support your pedagogy and will even help you improve it. Now, let's explore MathPlay!

REFLECTION QUESTIONS

1. What is your math story?
2. How do you best engage your students?
3. How do you connect with your students beyond the content you teach?

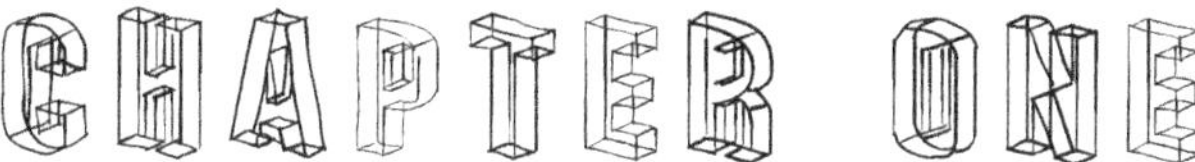

TEACHING IS ONLY DEMONSTRATING THAT IT IS POSSIBLE.
LEARNING IS MAKING IT POSSIBLE FOR YOURSELF.

PAULO COELHO

THE IDEA OF MATHPLAY

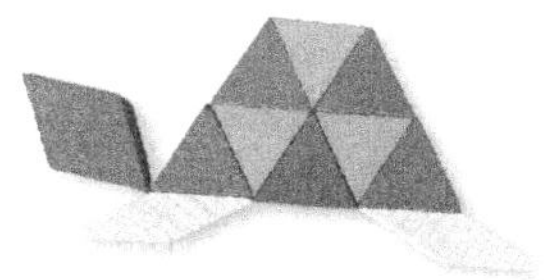

TO BE COMPLETELY HONEST, being a teacher is the second most important job I have. The first is being "Tata" (what both my daughters call me); Mariana is seven and in first grade and Madeline is two and pretty much does whatever she wants. Think about your own childhood or children you have been around recently. What is one thing young children love to do? Take three seconds, 3...2...1, Play! Yes, young children always want to play, any day of the week and any time of day is a great time to play. Children don't need a reason or specific directions when it comes to play. Playing comes natural to them and helps them explore the world around them. In addition, it seems like young children have unlimited energy levels and a built-in natural curiosity when it comes to play.

With this in mind, I have been using playtime to teach my daughters. As you can imagine, I really enjoy teaching math to my first grader. We have many different games and sets involving numbers, memory, shapes, patterns, and operations. We have both been enjoying MathPlay since she was in Pre-K. We often find ourselves doing MathPlay around the house, but most of the time we go down to our basement, otherwise known as MathPlay Headquarters.

One of my goals during MathPlay has always been for my daughter to explore concepts on her own, to try to discover if something is possible or not. When we first began exploring with MathPlay, she would sometimes get frustrated and request immediate help. Without giving her an answer, I would explore with her, modeling that it's okay to not know and it's also completely okay to make mistakes while exploring. I wanted her to feel empowered to try different approaches and to take as long as she needed. I believe children learn more from what they see us do than from what they hear us say.

When Mariana was younger, we started playing games that would strengthen her memory and focus. I'm a big fan of Dan Finkel's *Tiny Polka Dot* card game. We loved laying down the cards taking turns to make pairs of numbers and quantities as we revealed two at a time. It was a great way to spark mathematical conversations and to expose her to different numeric and graphic representations of different quantities.

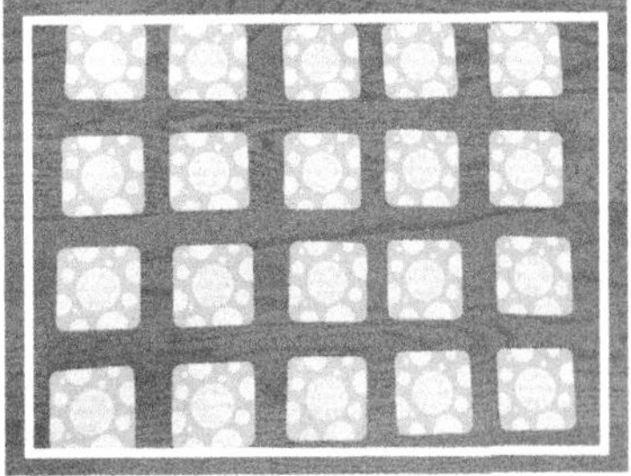

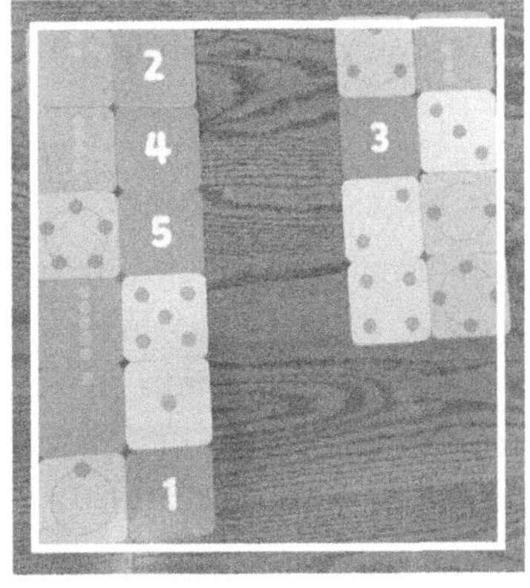

As she became more comfortable playing with the cards, we started using them to explore addition and subtraction. I would give her a card and ask her to find two cards that added up to that number or quantity. Then we would do it again so we could explore different paths to get to the same solution. We also started using other manipulatives like dice and dominoes. She became very good at this game so we began to explore higher numbers that she hadn't yet learned in school. It was a natural progression based on her ability and curiosity.

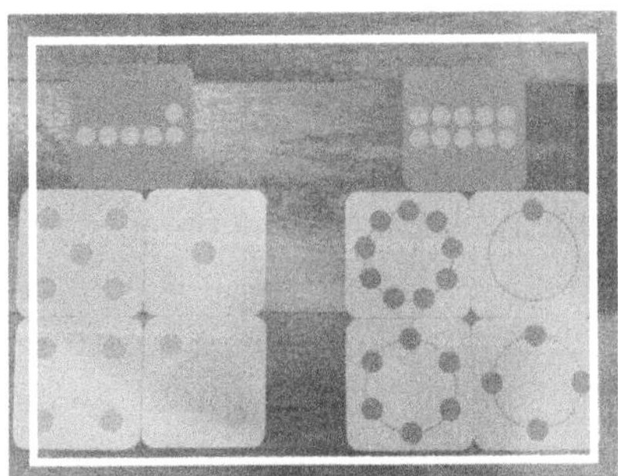

One activity she really enjoys is playing with patterns and shapes. Exploring different shapes is probably one of the most engaging ways to MathPlay with your kids or students. We started by playing simple games like making and labeling all the shapes she knew. At the time, she was learning some of these in school, so it was nice to be able to reinforce what she was learning at school in the context of MathPlay at home.

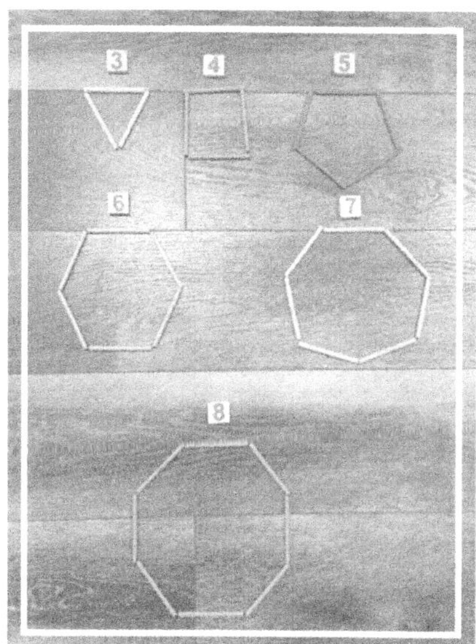

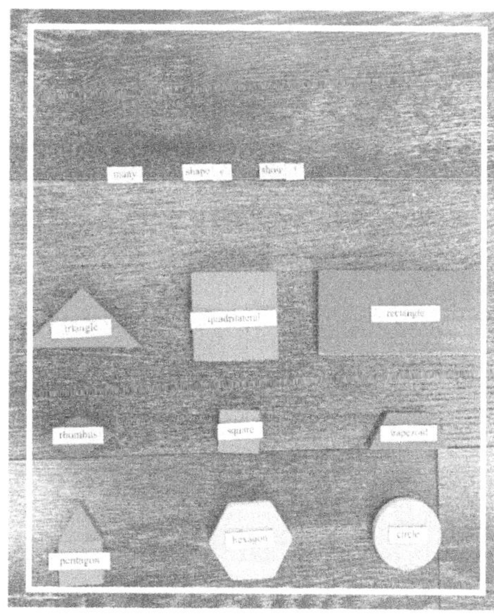

Our explorations led to learning about new shapes and even making some of her own. This was one of her favorite activities. She was always happy and engaged whenever we would MathPlay with shapes.

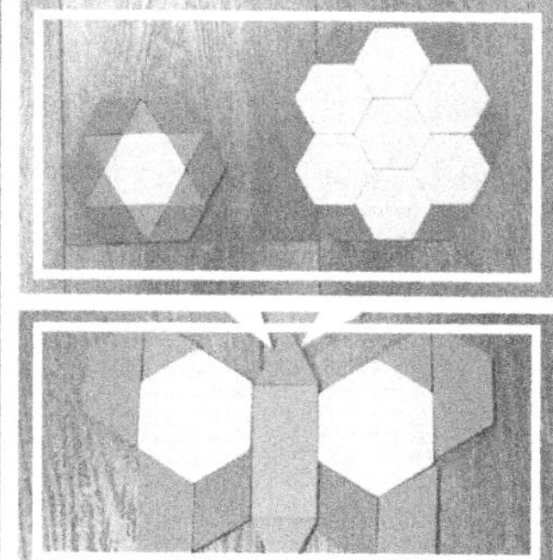

For these activities, we used sets from *Melissa and Doug* as well as the Deconstructing Geometry Magnet Set from *Public Math.*

One of my favorite MathPlay activities to explore with my daughter was building something two dimensional and then trying to translate it to three. Truth be told, she found this challenging and it wasn't always her favorite activity. Whether we were able to translate the shape into 3D or not, trying to was a great activity to explore and visualize objects in space. She was also able to rotate and translate shapes in the context of MathPlay which was somewhat unexpected but awesome to watch.

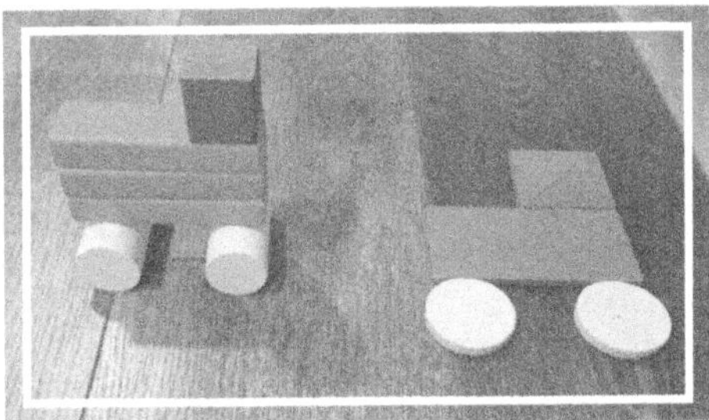

As time went on, I started to notice her becoming more comfortable trying to figure out things she did not know how to do on her own. She also started asking more questions while she was exploring. "Tata, what if we do this first?" "Tata, can we use Legos?" "Tata, can we try again?" "Tata, can you help me just a little bit?" She started to have the initiative and began leading some of our explorations. It didn't always work, but think about all you have accomplished in your life. How many of those accomplishments happened on the first try? Learning and discovery takes time. Sometimes she was trying something that I knew was not going to work, like the 2D to 3D game. I felt that if I told her she might have remembered but if she discovered it herself then she wouldn't forget. It was not always easy to watch her struggle but that struggle is a necessary component of the learning process.

As educators, we are very good at getting information from the questions our students ask in class. Their questions are a "screenshot" of sorts of their thinking process. During our MathPlay sessions, I particularly enjoyed exploring Mariana's questions. Many times as a teacher, I had a plan in mind that would result in exploring a concept I thought to be important. However, my daughter was the most engaged when we were exploring her questions because they were relevant and important for her. Using MathPlay allowed us to explore her questions in the context of discovery. Such explorations occurred in a very friendly and natural environment without any pressures to be done within a predetermined time frame.

One morning right before the beginning of the spring, my daughter and I had the following exchange:

Mariana: Tata, the birds are back!
Me: Yes, you're right!
Mariana: Where are they going to live?
Me: Hmm…
Mariana: Can we build a house for them?
Me: Yes! What shapes do we need?

Our conversation turned into a little math project. We talked about what shapes were needed to make a house and then drew some sketches of them. We talked about how to put them together and then built the house. It was a fun activity that really didn't take too much time. By validating and exploring her question, we were doing more than MathPlay. She learned that her ideas are important and worth exploring.

Another night, Mariana was taking a particularly long time to get ready for bed. I was doing my best to speed things up and as she was brushing her teeth, she stared at me for a few seconds and asked, "Tata, what's a negative number?" I was so excited that I forgot that it was time for bed. I knew she hadn't learned about negative numbers in school yet so I did what any math teacher parent would have done. I got some paper, drew a number line, and showed her that negative numbers are to the left of zero. My daughter stared at the number line for a few seconds and said, "So, negative numbers are like Anakin, they're on the dark side." To which I replied, "Exactly!" At this point, I was running down to the basement to get Star Wars Legos with my wife asking what was going on. I shared that we're doing something very important, and that Mariana couldn't go to sleep just yet. After a brief discussion, some laughs, and at least thirty more minutes of staying awake, this was the end result of that night:

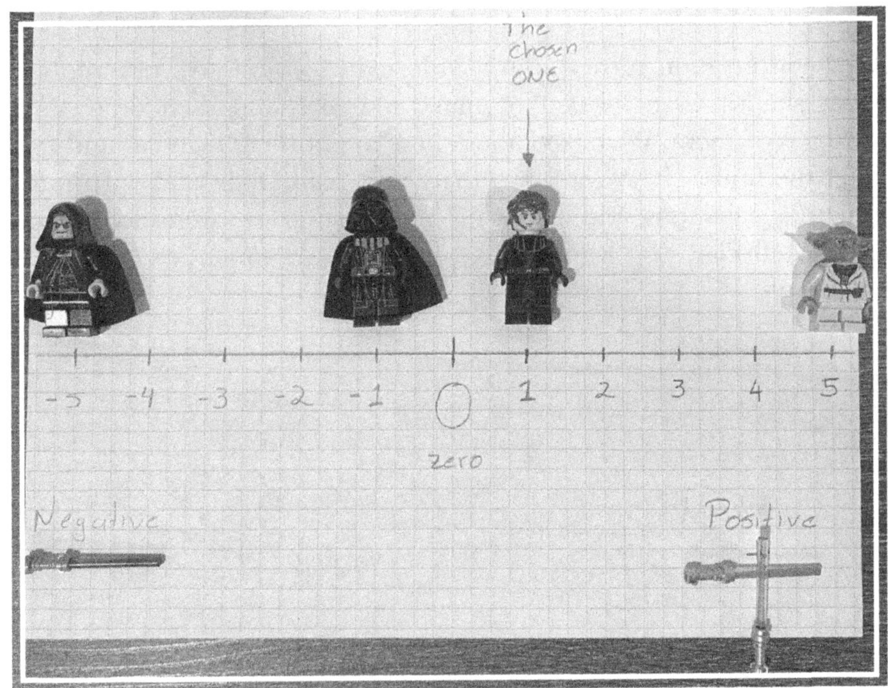

We talked about how Anakin was the chosen "ONE" but once he turned to the dark side, Darth Vader was right above negative one. She also made plus and minus signs using tiny lightsabers. We both enjoyed our conversation and using Legos to make math concepts more concrete. She still hasn't learned about negative numbers in school officially but got to explore them on her own through MathPlay.

For my daughter, MathPlay can sometimes be an excuse to stay awake a little longer. We both have really enjoyed the experience and have gained so much from it. Through MathPlay around the house, I learned that effective MathPlay has three main components: curiosity, exploration, and it is student-driven. There was always a question we were trying to figure out through exploration. It was also important for me to step back and let her take the lead. As a teacher (and her dad), it was hard not to help her as soon as she requested or needed help, however, I believe she's now more confident to try things on her own as a result. I believe that during our MathPlay explorations, we normalized that learning takes time and that making mistakes is part of that journey.

Whenever Mariana was enjoying MathPlay at home, I noticed she was naturally engaged on the task; she genuinely wanted to figure out a solution. As time went by, she would also attempt different strategies and methods without me giving her any specific directions. Her learning was not attached to a grade or bound by any time constraints (other than bedtime). Her learning was organic. Many times when I get home from work, she is waiting to tell me a story. She is always super excited to share and it usually goes like this, "Today in class, we were learning about ________, and I knew how to do it!" Sometimes, she'll even tell me she was able to help some of her classmates.

I believe that our MathPlay sessions have contributed to her love for learning new things and also sharing what she knows. I'd also like to mention that I have no formal training or experience teaching elementary students (other than my own daughter); many of our activities have been based on interests and intuition. Of course, I'm passionate about mathematics, but I don't think we need any particular training to MathPlay with our little ones at home. You don't have to be a chef to pretend you are cooking and eating food with your little ones nor do you have to be a doctor to play *Doc McStuffins.*

The idea of children learning through play is certainly not new to education or unique to a specific subject. In his theory of cognitive development, Jean Piaget describes different stages where children are active learners who use their experiences to develop their understanding of the world around them. According to Piaget, children engage in types of play that reflect their level of cognitive development: functional play, constructive play, symbolic/fantasy play, and games with rules (Johnson, Christie & Wardle 2005). Play is such a powerful human activity. During our MathPlay sessions my daughter has continued to develop many important skills beyond her math skills.

In order for us to figure out the best strategy to approach a MathPlay activity, we had to collaborate and communicate. She had to express her ideas, sometimes more than once, then be able to listen to feedback or a different strategy so she could decide how to move forward. Part of my goal was to provide her with enough information so that she could decide how to best approach a problem instead of just giving her a set of directions to follow. On many occasions, she did not agree with my ideas so she would say something like, "Tata, first we'll try this and then we can try your way." As her dad and an educator, it has been incredible to see her growth as a problem solver. From the beginning where she was waiting for me to help her get started to now where she is very comfortable sharing what she thinks we should do first.

My daughter has definitely learned important math concepts via MathPlay, however, the context of MathPlay has allowed her to develop critical skills that go beyond mathematics. For example, effective communication and collaboration are two skills my daughter is going to use beyond the school setting. I also believe that since our tasks were goal oriented (we're trying to solve a problem) she was also learning how to be a part of a team. Whether you think about elementary, secondary, college, or the workplace, how important is it for an individual to be able to collaborate and communicate with others?

The language my daughter used during our exchanges always gave me some insights to her mathematical understanding of the task at hand. Sometimes her ideas were right on point while on other occasions I was able to identify misconceptions. Either way, during our

MathPlay activities she always had the opportunity to test out her ideas for the purpose of discovery. I believe that is one of the keys about MathPlay, exploration, and discovery: setting the stage so that the learner can figure out the task at hand without a specific set of instructions to follow. In all honesty, this is not the way I learned math as a kid. My first memories of math take place in a very traditional setting, following directions from my dad or my teachers in school, and then doing significant repetition to sharpen my skills. If this method "worked" with me, why not use it with my daughter?

We still use repetition to practice specific skills like addition that requires carrying or subtraction that requires borrowing. There is value in the traditional method many of us experienced as students, however, MathPlay can be as effective. A recent study by the University of Cambridge analyzed the impact of teaching children aged three to eight through guided play. The study involved 3,800 children who experienced playful educational activities with the freedom to explore a learning goal in their own way. The study found that guided play can be just as effective as more traditional methods of class instruction and suggested that children "may master some skills better–notably in maths–more effective through guided play than any other method." I have to thank my Twitter friend, Stacey Roshan (@buddyxo) for sharing this amazing study with me. I honestly feel that using a MathPlay approach can be very appealing to most children. I also firmly believe that if we use more MathPlay in our classrooms, society's negative perception of mathematics will change. Instead of passing on our math anxiety to children, let's give them the opportunity to MathPlay.

As a mathematics educator, I started to wonder if this type of learning could happen in my high school math class. I wasn't sure if this approach would work with teenagers who are graded and follow a predetermined curriculum. Teaching one first grader in the comfort of our home was very different from teaching high schoolers in a school building. However, after experiencing the many benefits MathPlay had with Mariana, I felt that it could be a good idea, or at the very least an idea worth trying out. Truth be told, I had many doubts and worries about trying MathPlay at the secondary level. I was worried about three things, the first being trying something new without really knowing if it was going to work. Second, as many educators are, I was afraid to give up control. Effective MathPlay has to be student-driven which requires the teacher to step back, allowing students to lead. Lastly, my biggest fear was lack of student engagement. Personally, engaging students with mathematics really fuels my passion for teaching so this was an important concern for me. What if the idea of MathPlay was not as effective for secondary students as it was with my first grader at home?

As you can probably imagine at this point, while you are holding *Math Play* in your hands, I decided to give it a try. The results of facilitating MathPlay at the secondary level consistently surpassed any expectation I had. I even ended up using MathPlay with my college students, experiencing similar results with them. This book is a story from an educator that will hopefully inspire other educators to facilitate more MathPlay in their classrooms, schools, and homes. I want you to know that my journey of MathPlay was not a perfect one. There were times when things did not work as planned, but even on those days my students were engaged.

You can think of this book as a practical guide with specific examples and tools that will help you get started facilitating MathPlay with your students.

REFLECTION QUESTIONS

1. What were your favorite games to play as a kid?
2. What is your favorite game to play that involves math?
3. What are some of your kids'/students' favorite games?

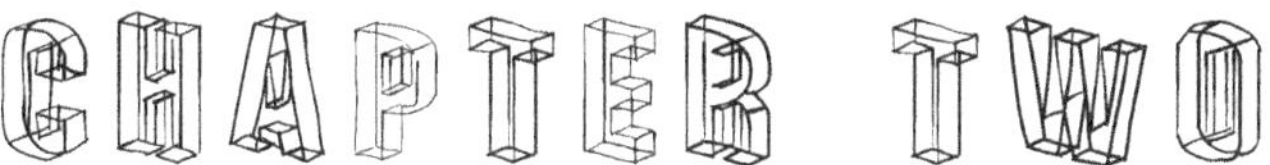

WHATEVER SUBJECT YOU TEACH, OR WHATEVER PART OF EDUCATION YOU'RE RESPONSIBLE FOR, YOU MUST FIND A WAY TO MAKE IT RELEVANT AND ENGAGING TO KIDS.

CHRIS WOODS

WHY DO WE NEED MORE MATHPLAY IN SCHOOLS?

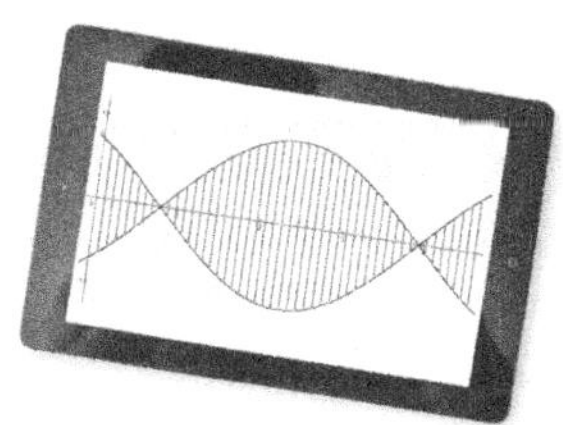

AT THIS POINT, YOU may agree that facilitating MathPlay with your little ones at home may be fun and worth trying out. You may even consider that there is plenty of room and opportunities for MathPlay at the elementary levels. Play is still very important in the life of our elementary learners but what about our secondary students? Do we really need MathPlay at the secondary level? Is there room or time for it? Generally speaking, students "playing" at the secondary level is not always perceived as an activity conducive of learning.

Regardless of the grade level you teach or your own feelings about math, consider the following questions as objectively as you can. In your opinion:

What percentage of students **truly** enjoy math class?

Is math class **only** enjoyable for students who perform well in it?

I imagine you did not answer 100% to the first question, while the second one could have gone either way. During the course of my career, I've had the opportunity to teach a wide range of subjects from pre-algebra to calculus. I have also taught different levels within each class, from essential to honors. Regardless of the level or performance, not enough students are truly enjoying math class on a daily basis across classrooms worldwide. As an educator in the role of a classroom teacher, I'm well aware that there are decisions made for us that have a direct impact on what happens in our classrooms. Most of the time teachers must tailor their instruction to meet curriculum requirements, time constraints, and end of the year assessments (just to name a few). It's possible to think we don't have time to MathPlay in secondary schools and that's why we shouldn't do it. However, if we embed MathPlay into the lessons we're already doing, then there is no need to find the precious extra time none of us really have.

Many times when I have shared a MathPlay activity (via Twitter mostly), I've gotten feedback that sounds like, "That's cute, but I don't have time for it." "I have been teaching like this for _____ number of years, why change it now?" "I'm not as familiar with that tech tool." and "That wouldn't work with my class/students." This feedback is valid and real; in all honesty my response is often something along the lines of "My students loved it and were very engaged." My decision to facilitate MathPlay in my classroom is centered around what I think is best for my students; I wholeheartedly believe that through MathPlay, students can learn mathematics purposefully. I would also love for my daughters to be able to MathPlay in their math classes until their high school senior year. There are opportunities for all of us, as educators, to facilitate MathPlay despite our time and curriculum limitations.

We shouldn't think of MathPlay as a "cute" one day activity that has little mathematical value. It also shouldn't be an isolated activity about a topic with no relation to what students are learning in class. Our students are very smart, they will quickly realize whether their MathPlay experience is authentic or not, and if it's not, they won't be completely engaged and we would have missed an opportunity. In more mathematical terms, MathPlay ≠ Busy Work. In this book, we will be exploring examples of MathPlay that involve rich and rigorous mathematical content at different levels. Learning rich mathematics and having fun are not mutually exclusive. In my experience, facilitating MathPlay can help students develop a deeper appreciation for mathematics and empower them to better understand it. The fact that you're reading this book tells me at the very least, you're interested in the idea of MathPlay and potentially giving it a shot.

In the past fourteen years working as a math teacher, I have learned so much from colleagues who were always willing to share some of their awesomeness and expertise. Brian Aspinall often says, "Sometimes the greatest PD is the teacher down the hall." I bet you thought of someone right after reading that line. Learning from another teacher's perspective can be incredibly powerful and even under similar conditions we may have very different experiences. It's quite possible that two teachers in the same school or department feel very different about their teaching experience. However, I believe there is one major pillar that is common to all educators, the GCF (Greatest Common Factor) of teaching. We all want to do what's best for our students. Our students should be at the center of every decision made in school, considering their input should always be a top priority since every decision educators make has a direct impact on how students get to experience school.

I believe that to get a better understanding of why we need more MathPlay in school, we need to hear from students. Everything we do in our classrooms should be centered around them. It makes perfect sense to include them in the conversation. Over the years, I've learned that students can provide feedback that can be transformative to any educator who wants to listen to it and implement it. I really wish that teaching programs could provide new teachers with more tools in how to seek out student feedback during the first years in the profession. It took me many years to feel comfortable enough to reach out to students for feedback. Earlier in my career, to be honest, I felt that seeking out student feedback may have been perceived as a deficiency. I now know that students are amazing at providing feedback and letting us know what works best for them and what does not. We should be utilizing their feedback regardless of where we are in our teaching careers.

With this in mind, I asked two former students a few questions about their experience in my class during their junior (eleventh grade) year. At the time they completed the questions, both students were seniors (twelfth grade) and had different math teachers.

STUDENT 1: NAILAH ELLIOT

WHAT IS THE MOST SIGNIFICANT THING YOU LEARNED/TOOK FROM MY CLASS?

I learned not to take failure or mistakes too hard. If I had dwelled on the mistakes I made in the beginning of the year and let the grades get to me too much, I probably wouldn't have had the strength or opportunity to get better and eventually succeed. This skill has helped me tremendously in my approach to other classes, and I am sure I will take it with me to classes in college and in the future.

WHAT ARE YOU MOST PROUD OF IN REGARDS TO YOUR WORK IN MY CLASS?

I am most proud of my consistency in performance for the second, third, and fourth quarters. Math is my favorite subject and my performance in those quarters definitely reflected that. I am also proud of my retained curiosity for solving complex problems even as the topics get harder and harder. Even though the problems don't always come immediately, I genuinely like being able to come to solutions. This class has taught me to think of math as less of a competition, which is how I had been accustomed to see it, and more of an ongoing pursuit of skills and ways to solve complex problems.

WHAT ARE YOUR THOUGHTS ON MATHPLAY?

I love the concept of MathPlay. I've always enjoyed math classes, simply because I love solving puzzles, but that does not mean the classes have always been fun. Even for a person who likes the subject matter, I have found myself dreading math classes from time to time because it is not always presented in a fun or digestible way. However, MathPlay completely destroys this concept. In hindsight, I always looked forward to precalc because of MathPlay. I knew each class would be different and the important concepts we needed to learn would be integrated into interesting and innovative activities, like the Pringleringle or the Desmos/Geogebra drawings. I really hope MathPlay will be utilized in more courses, especially for younger students. Oftentimes younger kids believe their lack of interest in math classes equates to their lack of interest in math itself–which is not true. With MathPlay, hopefully more students will see that math can be fun too!

STUDENT 2: CHARLES EMMANUEL

WHAT IS THE MOST SIGNIFICANT THING YOU LEARNED/TOOK FROM MY CLASS?

There are multiple ways to approach a problem. Although this applies to mathematics, it is also a lesson applicable to other aspects of life. When reviewing functions, for example, students observed three methods of completing a factoring problem. When doing math, being able to look at a problem in different ways is a very important skill that can help the mind grow. It also helps when discussing a topic as a group, for some people may look at a problem one way while others view it differently. Similarly, approaching things in life from different angles is integral to collaboration and development. I am glad that this lesson was taught and enforced throughout the course. I know that I will take it with me into the future and it will help me as it did in math.

WHAT ARE YOU MOST PROUD OF IN REGARDS TO YOUR WORK IN MY CLASS?

I am extremely proud of the work that I put into the class. I am most happy with my effort and ability to grow as a student. I really enjoyed the curriculum and felt very eager to learn. As a result, the year was full of me pushing myself and challenging the way that I think. I feel as though the variety in material allowed for me to gauge my brain in different ways and have me looking forward to learning each day.

WHAT ARE YOUR THOUGHTS ON MATHPLAY?

I think of MathPlay as a way to reach all students by making a curriculum that is both informative and engaging. Each classroom contains students with various learning styles and levels of engagement, but MathPlay unites everybody, giving everyone a rich learning experience. MathPlay is a memorable experience that allows all students to interact with the material in different ways; it can be used to start a unit or culminate it when reviewing for a test. Through the use of MathPlay, students can enter a class excited to have fun and leave for the day with new information about mathematics.

If you are an educator, you know that what you are teaching goes well beyond your content area. Just like Nailah and Charlie, I want all of my students to learn to approach problems from different angles, to persevere, and to have a growth mindset. This is not something we should be telling our students, instead, we should be modeling it for them. It really does not make sense for educators to encourage a growth mindset in our students while teaching them the way they were taught. I'm not arguing that the way we were taught was ineffective or that there have been significant changes in the mathematics our children are learning. However, students today live in a very different world. Just think of the technology they have at their fingertips and how easy it is to access information.

Growing up I remember my grandpa saying, "En lo poquito, se ve lo mucho," which translates to "You can see a lot in the little things." Our students are always learning from the little things we do (or don't do) in our classrooms. The way we interact with students and the way we handle and model mistakes are two examples that come to mind. Facilitating MathPlay in the classroom sends the message that we want to give our students a more enjoyable experience while teaching them the content they need to learn. This is something our students will appreciate and look forward to. It is also something that they will remember when they leave our classrooms. Many times, when I've run into a former student and we talked about class, they share happy memories about a specific lesson or problem we did that was meaningful to them. I bet every teacher can relate. Facilitating MathPlay in the classroom can help create more of those happy memories in math class. As a math educator, wouldn't you want more people to appreciate math the way you do? I think we would be contributing to changing society's negative perception of mathematics.

Our students can easily tell whether we care more about them or the content we teach. They know when we put a little extra effort into our lessons. We, as teachers, are responsible for knowing our content and deciding how to deliver it. Facilitating MathPlay can make math class a more enjoyable experience for all of our learners, regardless of the class or level. Students will be very engaged and more willing to try when they are doing MathPlay in the classroom. Bringing MathPlay in our classrooms will also contribute to student ownership of the material and community building (more on that later).

So, why do we need more MathPlay in schools? Consider the following benefits:

HIGHER LEVELS OF ENGAGEMENT

Facilitating MathPlay provides a context in which students can apply the mathematical concepts they are currently learning in class. Students are able to demonstrate mastery of their learning while having some level of choice. More often than not, our MathPlay activities require student collaboration and the use of different available technologies. I've noticed that students really appreciate the opportunity to be creative and collaborate in math class. Regardless of the level of the class I was teaching (essential, standard, or advanced), I honestly cannot think of a single time when students complained or were not engaged in a MathPlay activity.

CHANGF NEGATIVE PERCEPTION OF MATH CLASS

This one really goes beyond the classroom. Many of our high school students have this already set idea of where they stand in mathematics. Basically, they're good at math or they're not. Facilitating MathPlay for students can help them realize that there is way more to math than "good" or "bad." There is a place in mathematics for all of our learners. I strongly believe that math class has the potential to be every student's favorite class. What would happen if students started to come home to talk about how much fun they had in math class? We can make a small contribution to this transformative change by facilitating more MathPlay in our classrooms.

STUDENT-DRIVEN EXPERIENCE

When facilitating MathPlay, our goal as a teacher is for all of our students to arrive at the same destination. You, as the teacher, know what your students should be able to do by the end of the lesson. However, students may take a different path to get there as there is no specific set of instructions to follow that will get them to their destination. I'm not suggesting there is no teacher guidance whatsoever but it's important for students to have some level of choice in how to complete the task. A different path can certainly be a different mathematical approach to solve a quadratic equation or prove that a quadrilateral is a parallelogram for example. However, a different path may also be a longer path, where students can move at their own pace. Using different paths is very natural when facilitating MathPlay and because there is a level of choice it frees students from comparing their individual process to that of their peers.

CREATING MORE HAPPY MEMORIES IN MATH CLASS

The opportunity to play and collaborate with others sets the stage for creating happy memories in math class. When students are given a chance to apply their math knowledge with a purpose, there is a very positive classroom atmosphere. There is no sense of competition, which in my experience can be very common in advanced/honors classes. There is also an understanding of each students' uniqueness as students are able to arrive at the learning goal using different paths, and that's okay.

These are just four of the many benefits of facilitating MathPlay with our students. There are more benefits, both direct and indirect, that we will explore in the upcoming chapters. My hope is that at this point you have a clear reason for why you want to try MathPlay with your students. Personally, I want my class to be the most engaging class my students have ever taken. I'm not suggesting in any way it is, it's more of an aspiration. My reason for MathPlay is directly related to what I think is best for my students. Why do **you** want to facilitate MathPlay?

There will be times when not facilitating MathPlay may seem easier or better. When that happens, go back to your answer from the questions above. Based on what I have learned, facilitating MathPlay with my high school students was as effective as it was with my own daughter. Just like my daughter, my students loved the idea and were completely engaged anytime we had an opportunity to MathPlay. I'm very happy to share that my students at all levels (essential, standard, and advanced) were all equally engaged in our MathPlay activities.

Facilitating MathPlay at home with my daughter was relatively easy because of the context and all the freedoms we had, however, doing it at the high school level required a little more planning and preparation. Let's now explore how to get started with MathPlay in school.

REFLECTION QUESTIONS

1. Think about your own experience as a student and the students you teach. How are they similar but different?
2. What is one happy memory you have from math class as a student? What about as an educator?
3. What is one thing you do in the classroom to change the negative perception of mathematics?

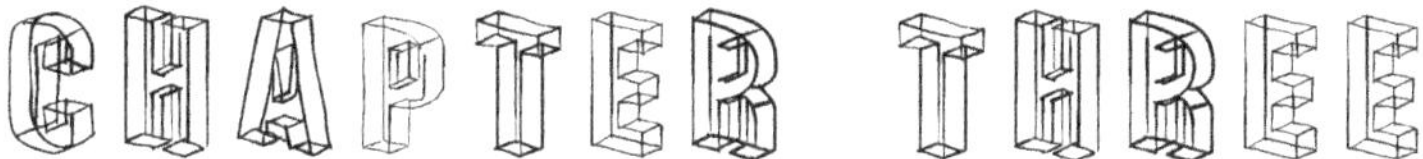

CHAPTER THREE

BUILDING COMMUNITY IN MATHEMATICS INVOLVES DEVELOPING COLLABORATIVE SKILLS THAT DIMINISH HIERARCHIES. SUCCESSFUL COLLABORATIONS ARE INCLUSIVE AND BENEFIT FROM DIVERSE VIEWPOINTS.

FRANCIS SU

GETTING STARTED WITH MATHPLAY

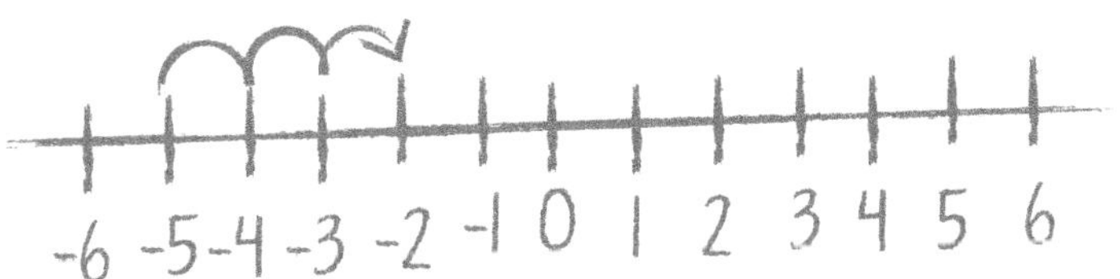

THINKING ABOUT OUR LINE of work as educators, do you remember what your first year lessons looked like? How different are those lessons from the ones you are currently using? Regardless of how many years we have been teaching, there is always room for improvement and every new school year I strive to be a better teacher than the previous year. I feel that as we start gaining experience, we become more comfortable and effective with how we run our classes. Facilitating MathPlay in my classroom required me to do things differently. I had to make changes to some lessons I'd always considered to be effective.

The adage, "If it ain't broke, don't fix it" was what went through my head during this time. However, if everyone used that thinking model, we would still be walking and using horses to get to places. I wondered if I should change something I knew worked for something that may not have. After my MathPlay experience with my daughter, I felt it was definitely worth the shot. Truth be told, I was worried about giving up control of the lesson as effective MathPlay must be student-driven. I was also worried about lack of student engagement. What if the idea of MathPlay did not resonate with my high school students?

At the time I was teaching geometry, algebra 2, precalculus, and calculus. I had to decide where and how to start with MathPlay at the secondary level. I had the feeling that my geometry class would probably be a good place to start. It's worth mentioning that I have taught geometry multiple times at different levels, i.e., essential, standard, and advanced, so I'm very comfortable and familiar with both the content and the pace of the class. There are multiple opportunities in geometry to make connections to everyday life. When discussing shapes, size, distance, and position students can use the knowledge they are learning in class and apply it beyond the classroom. At the time, my geometry students were learning about right triangles. This is a topic they have seen in the past that is related to other topics like equations, slope, and angles. I felt that right triangles would be a great opportunity to facilitate MathPlay.

I already had a lesson built over the years that I wanted to use. It did not make sense for me not to use it given that our students benefit from our past experiences (both good and bad), I simply needed to embed MathPlay to the lesson I already had. Facilitating MathPlay does not imply that you have to create a completely new lesson for a topic you have already taught in the past. However, making some changes to the lesson you already have can have a very positive impact on how students engage with the topic. I ended up changing how students would complete their independent practice. In my original lesson, I had different practice problems covering different scenarios students could encounter later on. Instead of completing those problems, I asked students to find an object that looked like a right triangle, take a photo of it to then prove or disprove that it was actually a right triangle. It wasn't a significant change in the lesson and it also did not take a lot of work to change or prepare for it.

After we had completed the first part of the lesson, I asked my students to walk around their house (we were learning remotely as this was early into the pandemic) to find an object that looked like a right triangle, take a photo of it and come back. I remember that on this particular day, we all looked like we needed a break from the screen and so I gave them ten minutes for the task. I was nervous that a student may come back to share they couldn't find anything or even worse, not come back at all. I admit that giving up control of the class is not easy to do. After about what felt like five very long minutes, students started to come back to share their photos. We all got to see many potential right triangles. From that moment, I noticed students were eager and excited to share their photos with the rest of the class.

I did not have to call on anyone to share, there was a natural flow. Students even started commenting on each other's photos.

At this point in the lesson, I asked students to upload their photo to *GeoGebra* and then prove or disprove whether it was a right triangle or not. Using *GeoGebra* allowed students to have coordinates for the vertices so they could measure different angles and segments. I purposely did not give students many specific directions because I wanted them to have some level of freedom in what method or strategy they would use. My students were really excited. Some required support uploading their photos but for the most part it ran very smoothly. Another very positive aspect of the lesson was that when students needed support, other students jumped in to help. In my experience our students are probably the best tech support we could ever have.

Here is a sample from a student where he went outside to take a photo of his family's car:

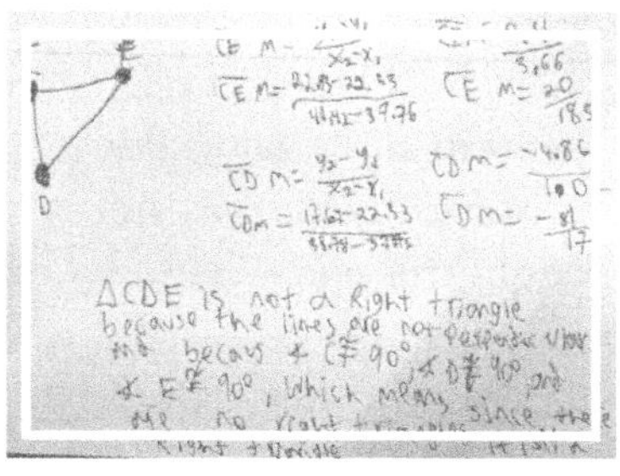

In this case, he decided to use slope formulas to find out whether there were perpendicular lines or not. He concluded it couldn't be a right triangle since none of the line segments were perpendicular to each other. If you look closely at the photo, you will notice he also used the angle measuring feature in GeoGebra to find if there was a right angle or not.

Here is another example where a student took a photo of a little triangle inside a weight scale:

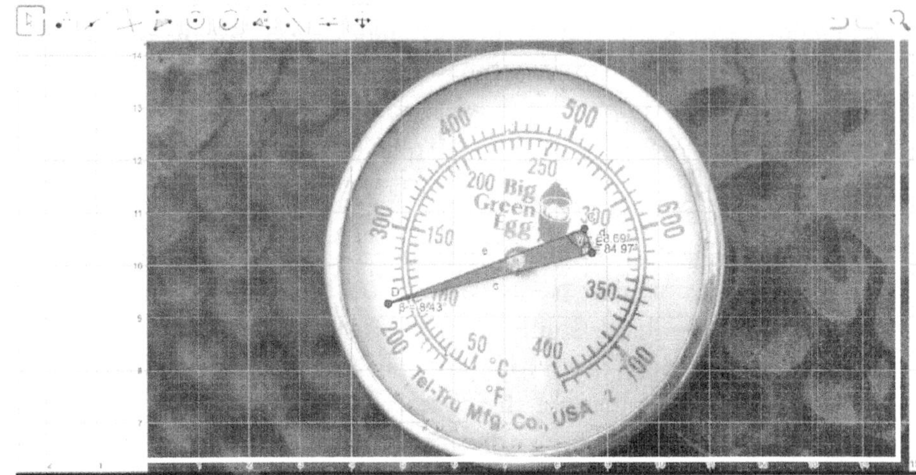

In this case they measured each angle of the triangle using GeoGebra and they also found the length of each side. Then, using the Pythagorean theorem they were able to prove that it was not a right triangle.

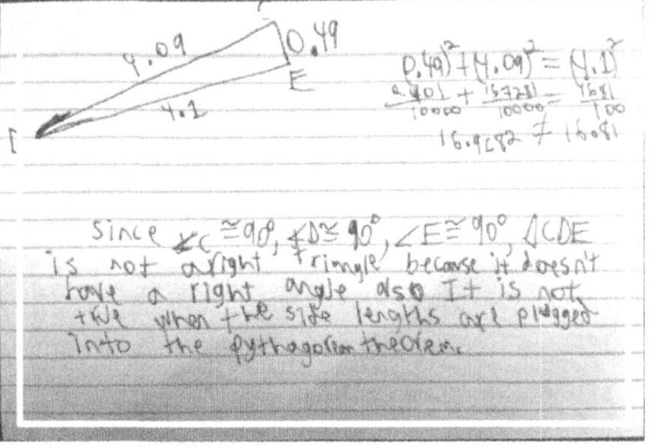

Here is the last sample of work where a student took a picture of the corner of a window frame:

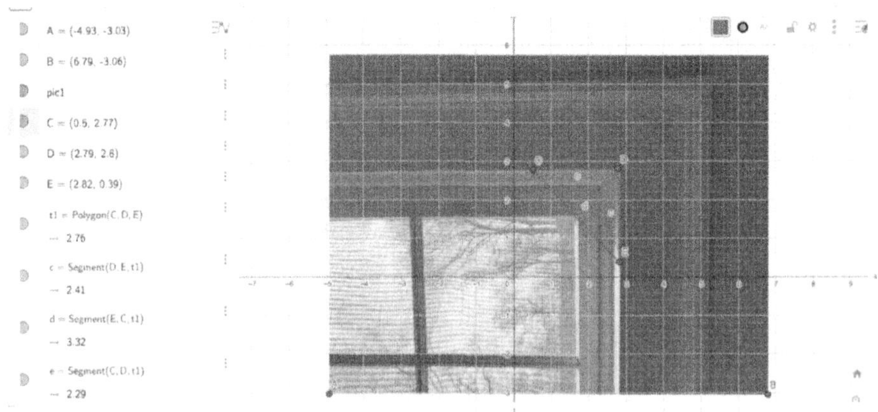

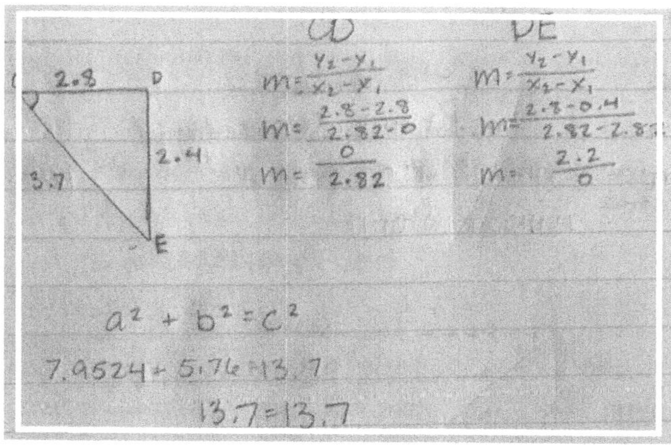

In this example, the student calculated the slopes and found out one to be zero and the other to be undefined. The student concluded the lines were horizontal and vertical respectively. Therefore, the lines were most definitely perpendicular to each other. The student also found the measurement of each side and used the Pythagorean theorem to prove that the triangle was a right triangle.

By just analyzing three different samples, we can notice how many connections were made by students on their own. Many students used multiple strategies for their problem. I was very happy to see they were making connections to the slope of a line, distance between two points, measuring angles, and of course the Pythagorean theorem. If we pause to think, every student did only one question. I was hesitant about not giving more practice problems. However, I learned that doing one meaningful question was as effective as doing multiple practice questions. The students also felt proud about displaying their work as there was a sense of ownership.

Reflecting back, I believe that starting with geometry was the right move for me. I feel that, if possible, you should start facilitating MathPlay in a class where you feel comfortable and have had some experience teaching. I would also not recommend grading the activity the first time you do it to ensure students are not worried about losing points over accuracy. Facilitating MathPlay should be an engaging tool that sparks creativity.

Seeing how engaged my geometry students were really made me feel that this could potentially work and be implemented in any of the classes I was teaching at the time. I started thinking about how to implement it with my precalculus students. It's definitely easier to implement MathPlay in some classes or for particular topics, however, if we are just waiting for the right topic or the right time to MathPlay, it's likely that it won't happen. The goal is to start implementing MathPlay in all the classes you're teaching for all topics.

At the time, my precalculus students were learning about conic sections. In full disclosure, I had taught conic sections before both in algebra 2 and precalculus so I had all the materials I needed. If you have taught conics, you know there are multiple formulas involving many variables for parabolas, circles, ellipses, and hyperbolas. Scrolling through my Twitter feed, I came across the Pringles Ringle challenge which had been around for a few years.

I couldn't help but notice that this was one of the shapes my students were studying in class. Had I found my MathPlay activity for conics? I started to gather information and looked up some tutorials on YouTube. I got myself some Pringles and began building the ring. It took three attempts. I realized this activity could be completed within a class period and it was both challenging and engaging.

Completing the Pringles Ringle challenge was definitely worth doing. I wanted to take it a step further and use it to make a deeper connection to the mathematics we were learning in the course. After students were able to build the circle, I asked them to take a photo of it and upload it to *Desmos* to find the equation for it. This is an activity your students will enjoy and always remember.

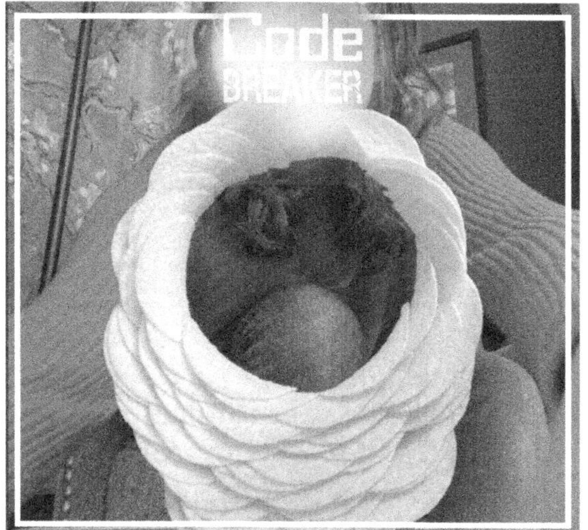

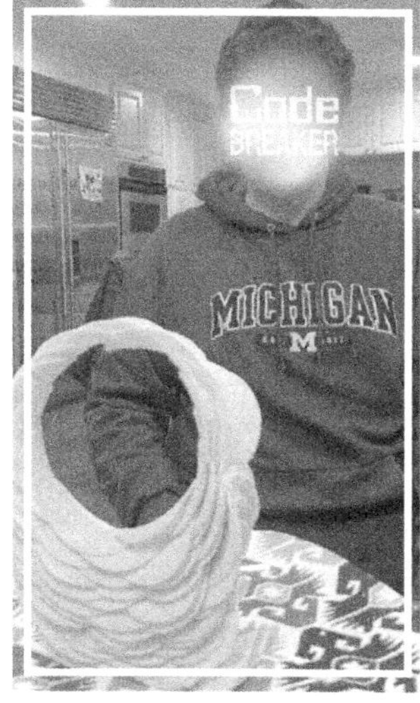

I have done the circles and Pringles activity in the classroom, remotely, and also as an independent assignment. Here are some of the things I have learned: the activity can be completed within a class period (45 - 60 minutes), you need a big can of Pringles per circle, but you should have extras (especially if you or your students like to eat them). It's not required that your students have used Desmos prior to this activity, although it can be helpful.

I also recommend modeling how to upload their photo to Desmos and providing them with a video tutorial of how to construct the circle. There are many available on YouTube. Scan the QR code to view the tutorial I use. It's very likely that your students won't be able to complete the circle on their first try, however, this is one of the reasons why this activity is both challenging and rewarding.

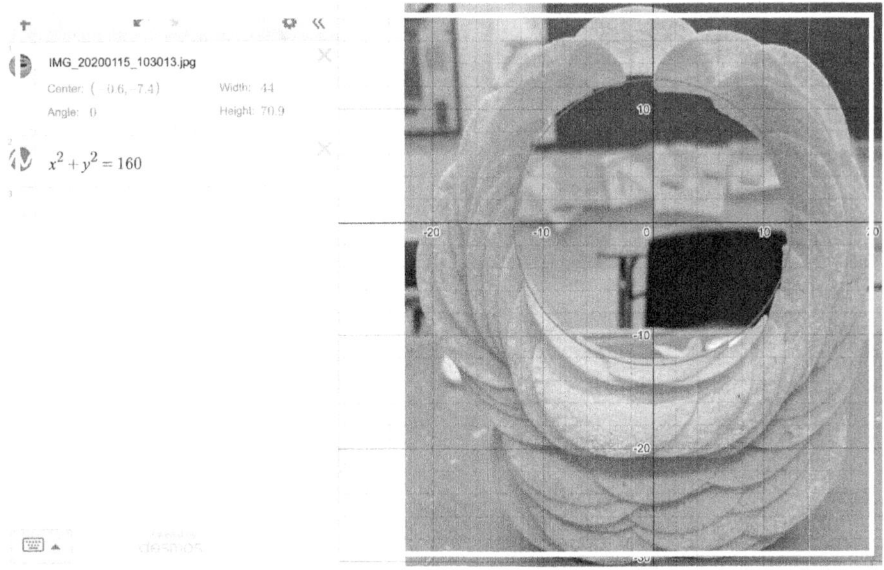

Another nice perk about this activity is that every time I have done it, there is always a student who shares that their circle came out looking more like an oval. Most of the time they're worried that their circle equation won't be a "perfect" fit. This is always an amazing conversation because it leads into ellipses which happens to be the next conic section we get to study. I really enjoy that this happens naturally, and the students notice that there is a need for a different shape. This was something I did not plan but am so glad it happened.

Facilitating MathPlay with my students was a very enjoyable and rewarding experience. I highlighted some of their amazing work on Twitter because I was really proud of them. While there are many opinions about social media use as educators, when I have posted student work, it has a special meaning for my students. They are happy and proud of their work. For this particular Pringles project, all of my students were completely engaged. There was a strong sense of purpose and ownership. When I was looking over their projects, it was very clear they gave me their best work and effort.

As I was walking around during the activity, I noticed that collaboration was necessary and happening all around. Different groups were coming up with strategies to try first, deciding the thickness of the base, how many cans were needed, who had the steadiest hands, etc. As a teacher, I don't think I could have given them a set of problems in a worksheet where they could have had such levels of collaboration. I'm not arguing that worksheets have no place in a math classroom, as a student I always felt I needed to complete all the questions on the worksheet to be best prepared for the test. Whether this was true or not, I believe that the process of completing the problems gave me endurance and also a degree of confidence.

After completing this activity with my precalculus students, I felt that it was possible to facilitate MathPlay in all of my classes. Of course, there are topics that are easier than others but with some planning it is possible to embed MathPlay into your current lessons. I also believe that we, as teachers, know what's best for our students. You may feel your students are not ready for a full MathPlay lesson and that's okay. You can certainly start small until you (and they) are more comfortable. It may also be a good idea to get some feedback from your students to get a sense of what topics (outside of school) they are interested in. Then, try to merge the roads of mathematics and their interests to your lesson.

As a classroom teacher, I recognize that we may not have a lot of free time. If you feel that making changes to your lessons is not a good place to start, maybe you can consider implementing non-curricular tasks. There are many already made resources and problems you can try with your students that can be very engaging and fun. This can be a safe way to start facilitating MathPlay in your classroom. After reading some of the work of Peter Liljedahl, I decided to try some of these problems with my students. To be honest, I chose problems based on what I was teaching so that my students wouldn't feel as if we were doing something random out of nowhere. During our unit of sequences and series, I gave my students the following problem:

Picture a Rubik's Cube. Now drop it into paint so that it covered. When the paint is dry, imagine smashing it on breaking it apart into smaller cubes.

1) How many of the cubes have one face covered in paint?
2) How many cubes have two faces covered in paint?
3) How many have three faces covered in paint?
4) How many have zero covered in paint?

Students worked in small groups to figure out a solution. While I did not provide many directions or much support along the way, students were able and encouraged to check in with other groups to get ideas and perspective. Students were able to collaborate and there was definitely knowledge mobility within the classroom. It was awesome to see different groups working together inside and outside the classroom.

In the photo, you'll notice there is a student in class collaborating with a classmate who is remote. This lesson took place during a period of hybrid instruction. Using non-curricular tasks can definitely be a safe way to give up some classroom control and see how students respond to having some of the initiative. It can give you a sense of how your students will behave in a less traditional setting. Allow your students to explore and enjoy mathematics without worrying about a grade. If you feel you need a grade, consider grading for completion.

Another fantastic option to try something different in class is using *Open Middle* by Robert Kaplinsky. Scan the QR code to find different problems organized by topics and grade levels. The problems can really give students a different perspective and a break from the routine. One of the things I particularly enjoy about open middle problems is that students almost always come up with different ways to approach the question. It's very important for our students to experience different paths to get to the same solution. Inspired by the work of Robert, I wrote this problem:

Directions: Use the digits from 0 to 9, at most one time each, to fill in the boxes to create a number with the following properties:

-The number formed by the first two digits is divisible by two
-The number formed by the first three digits is divisible by three
Repeat the process until you get to the last number

Write a paragraph explaining your strategy/method to figure out the number

They had a lot of fun trying to come up with the number. It turns out there's only one possible solution. Problems of this type can spark curiosity and creativity, setting the stage for MathPlay. It's also worth mentioning that many students chose to make a video instead of writing a paragraph, which I thought was fantastic. Seeing the levels of engagement of my students has really fueled my passion for teaching mathematics, and it has pushed my thinking in trying to find more ways to bring it to class.

I hope that at this point you are already thinking specifically about how you can start MathPlay with your students. Facilitating MathPlay with your students should not feel like something extra you now have to do. Instead, it should be seen as an opportunity to teach what they need to learn in a setting that is more student-driven and promotes creativity. Within the unit or chapter you are currently covering, is there an opportunity for you to facilitate MathPlay? If you think there isn't, maybe you can end the unit with a MathPlay review lesson. At this point, the students already have the content knowledge so it can be a great opportunity to apply it. Similarly, you can also start a unit with MathPlay to get a sense of what skills students have/need going into the chapter.

We may all be at different places in our career but all we need to do is take the first step towards facilitating MathPlay. I believe the most important step in every journey is the first step.

REFLECTION QUESTIONS

1. From the classes you're currently teaching, in what class do you feel it would be easier to start facilitating MathPlay?
2. As you think about MathPlay, is there a topic you have taught that comes to mind?
3. Can you think of a colleague in your school who may also be interested in facilitating MathPlay?

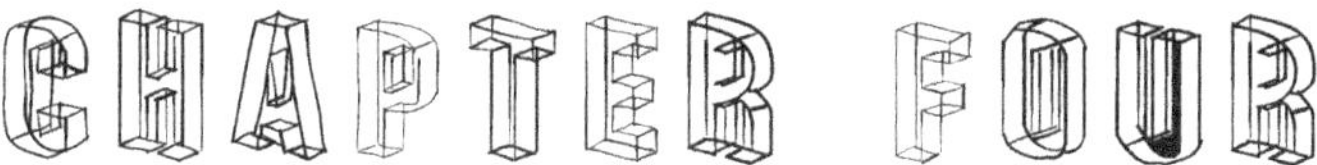

THE IMPORTANT THING TO REMEMBER ABOUT MATHEMATICS
IS NOT TO BE FRIGHTENED.

RICHARD DAWKINS

MATHPLAY IN ACTION

AS YOU START FACILITATING more MathPlay with your students or children at home, you will start to recognize and capitalize on more opportunities. On many occasions I thought to myself, "This is an impossible topic to facilitate any MathPlay," to later find out it was not only possible but also engaging and fun. Reflecting on my own journey, I wanted to share some of the things I found to be helpful with engaging in MathPlay.

KNOWING ABOUT STUDENTS' INTERESTS OUTSIDE THE CLASSROOM

Anything that peaks the interest of your students can be an engagement tool for you as an educator. I believe that learning about students beyond the classroom is completely relevant to all educators. This is an ongoing process that takes time. From the first day of classes to the last, we're always learning about our students. In my experience, students will be very appreciative of our lessons when they learn we related it to something of their interest. It really does not have to be something major or very time consuming, it can be something small with a powerful impact. I'll give you an example. Early in the school year, my geometry students were learning about the building blocks of geometry; this can be a dry lesson where they are learning many definitions involving points, lines, and planes.

I knew a couple of students played for the school soccer team because they wore their jerseys to class, and I heard them talking about past and upcoming matches. After going over the definitions, I gave them a picture of the Paris Saint-Germain FC formation, which included top soccer stars like Messi, Neymar, Mbappe, and Ramos just to name a few. By looking at this picture, the building blocks of geometry came alive. The plane was the field, the players the points, and there were multiple line segments (since they don't extend forever). Students also noticed the defenders played in a collinear formation. I didn't have to make any significant changes to my lesson or interview every student to find out what their interests were. I Googled "PSG formation" and added that picture to my lesson presentation. I like soccer myself and facilitating this discussion helped me connect with my students beyond the content we were learning. Needless to say, this example would work with any team sport your students play.

Objective: Identify and model points, lines, and planes

RELATING WHAT STUDENTS ARE LEARNING TO WHAT'S HAPPENING IN THE WORLD

This may sound a little overwhelming, but it does not have to be. We live in a world of social media trends and instead of restricting those conversations we should leverage them to our advantage. It's not easy but it's not impossible. For me it usually follows two questions: What's trending for them and how can I use it in our lessons? Once again, it doesn't have to be something that is very time consuming. Last year, many of my students (and myself) were hooked on Disney's *The*

Mandalorian. I remember they were very excited about the appearance of Ahsoka Tano in one of the episodes. Since we were going to learn about trigonometric ratios next, with a Google search I found the perfect image for this lesson relating trigonometric ratios to *Star Wars*. My students were really happy and excited to see that Ahsoka Tano had made it to our lesson.

IDEAS FROM TWITTER

I opened a Twitter account during the summer of 2019. For the first ten years of my teaching career I completely avoided social media. I felt that social media was the tool used for many teachers to get in trouble. Whether it was something they posted, commented, or liked, I felt (in my ignorance) that it was always something negative. Luckily I read *The Power of Branding: Telling Your School's Story* co-authored by Joseph Sanfelippo and Tony Sinanis. Reading this book and seeing some of the amazing work of my colleague Tony, really started to change my perspective about using social media as an educator. I learned it was a powerful tool and we get to decide how to use that tool. Personally, I use it to find inspiration and also as a digital window into my classroom.

I learned that educators on Twitter will generously share ideas and some of their expertise without expecting anything in return. Since I opened my account I have been learning so much from educators on Twitter. I have connected with amazing educators worldwide who have helped me grow both personally and professionally. I no longer see social media as a tool to get teachers in trouble but as a tool for professional development and growth. As a mathematics educator, I have found great ideas using the hashtags #MTBoS (Math-Twitter Blog-o-Sphere) and #iTeachMath. What usually happens is that I come across something that I'll save and use it later on.

My hope is that by sharing some of the things that work for me, it will inspire you to find what works best for you. I strongly believe that getting to know your students, using current events, and leveraging social media can help you facilitate more MathPlay in your classroom which can result in increasing student engagement. Now, let's take a look at some other examples in different contexts, classes, and levels.

MATHPLAY DURING THE HOLIDAYS

MathPlay is now something that my daughter and I get to constantly enjoy together. During the last winter break, she was very excited about Christmas. One morning while playing with our shapes set, my daughter said she wanted to create some Christmas decorations using the shapes. She was walking around the house looking at what shapes she wanted to try. After some attempts and with minor assistance from "Tata," she created these:

After we finished playing with the shapes, she asked, "Tata, what if we use the geoboard?" to which I replied, "Holy Guacamole, that's a great idea!" She was able to create another tree and a present. It was such a fun morning. I was really happy to see her so engaged playing with different shapes in the context of the holidays.

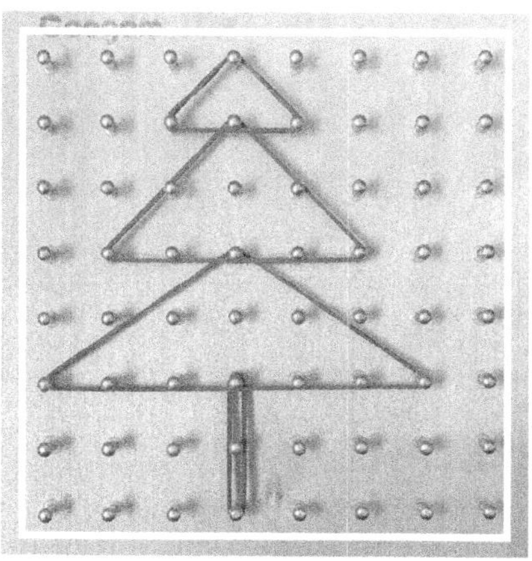

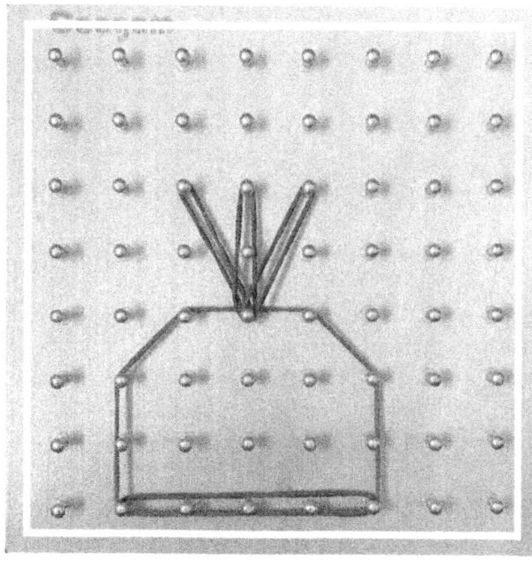

MATHPLAY WITH POLAR COORDINATES

Polar coordinates is usually a new topic for students in precalculus. One of the first things students learn to do is plot points using polar coordinates. Each point on the polar plane is determined by a distance from a reference point and an angle from a reference direction. The angles can be measured in either degrees or radians. In my experience, students are very comfortable using cartesian coordinates but not always when it comes to using polar coordinates.

With this in mind, I knew my students needed to practice plotting polar coordinates to become more comfortable with them. I have used worksheets in the past where students got to practice the concept; to be honest that's how I learned and got to practice a lot of the mathematics I learned in school. There is nothing wrong with having students practice with a worksheet, however, when doing so I feel students tend to be less engaged with the concepts they are learning.

This was a great opportunity for MathPlay! I started looking for ideas on how to make polar coordinates more engaging. I found a *GeoGebra* applet, courtesy of Daniel Mentrard, where students could play a game of Battleship using polar coordinates. In addition, students received immediate feedback as soon as they entered their coordinates.

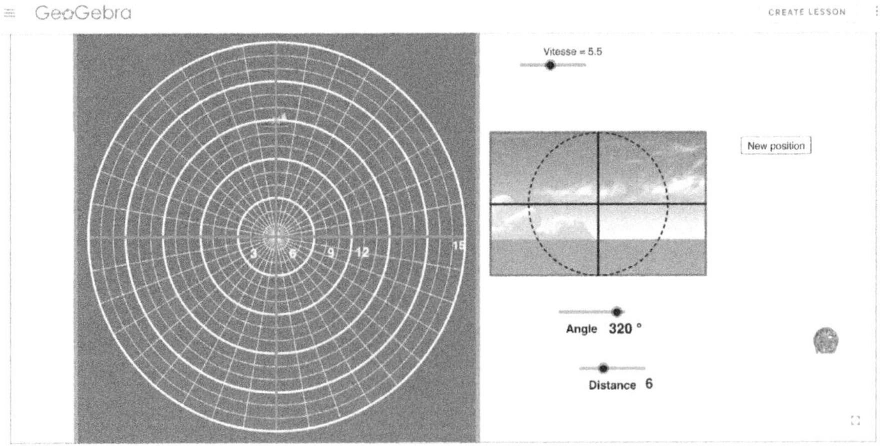

My students were extremely engaged and really got to enjoy the game. They were practicing how to plot polar coordinates, which they could have done on a worksheet, but their engagement level was fantastic. They started to time one another to see who could hit more targets in less time which required a solid understanding of polar coordinates. I learned that many students continued to play after class and also went back to the activity to review as we got closer to our assessment for that particular unit.

MATHPLAY WITH OPTIMIZATION

In my experience, one really fun unit to teach in calculus is optimization. Students get to apply their knowledge of derivatives in real world problems that require them to maximize (profit, area, volume, etc) or minimize (cost, materials, etc). Students get to use calculus in a different context that requires them to think outside the box. Ironically, one classic optimization problem deals with an open box in which students are given a rectangular shaped material, they are then asked to cut out equal squares from every corner to create an open box with the greatest possible

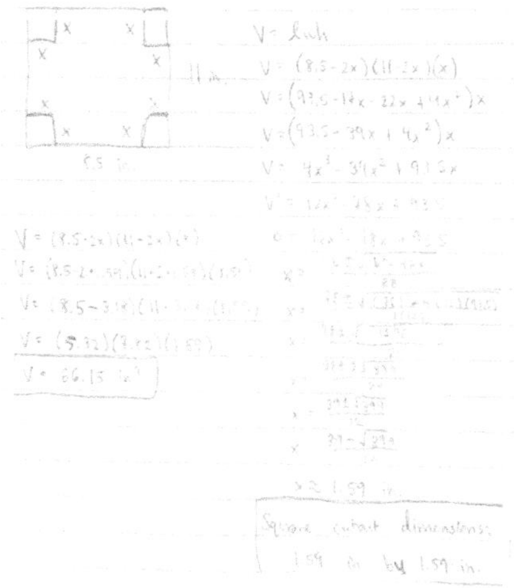

volume.

This is definitely a lesson where students can collaborate and use each other as learning resources. We did an example together as a class, then students did an independent problem using the dimensions of a letter sized paper.

While students were working on their independent practice, I used an animated *GeoGebra* applet, courtesy of Vincent Pantaloni, in which students could see the relation between the original piece of paper, the tangent line to the function, and its relation to the volume (all at once). Using this kind of technology can really help students get a deeper understanding of the concepts they are learning. It can really bring mathematics to life in the classroom by making concepts more concrete. Here is a link to the applet and a picture of what it looks like courtesy of @panlepan.

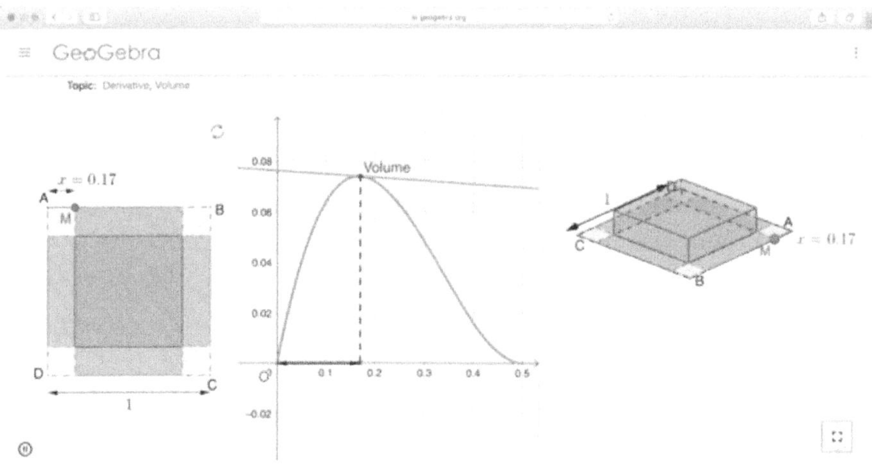

At this point, I felt students had a solid understanding and sense of purpose to our optimization lesson. They were now ready to MathPlay. I handed out a letter sized piece of paper to each student asking them to now make their own box and decorate it. They really enjoyed building their own box and I feel that the abstract portion of the lesson became very concrete for them. It was such a powerful lesson. I recognize that we spent a lot of time on one question, however, the students were really engaged and had a deeper understanding of what it meant to optimize the volume. There was also a sense of ownership over the work they were doing. They were all solving the same question, but every student got to decorate their own box.

MATHPLAY MEETS ART

One of my favorite MathPlay activities involves having students create a *Desmos* art project. This is a project that can be tailored to any math class, from an algebra class where students can use lines with different slopes to create their drawings to precalculus students who can go way beyond linear functions. The first time my students completed a *Desmos* art project was in a precalculus class. We had just finished polynomial and rational functions and it was a great opportunity to apply the knowledge they had gained in a different context. As *Desmos* art projects are very popular, I wanted to limit the possibility of students finding (and potentially just copying) a project that was already made. I felt that it would probably be a good idea to center the project around our school spirit at Horace Greeley High School in Chappaqua, NY.

Students took a picture of something that resembled school spirit then recreated that picture on *Desmos* using different types of functions as well as multiple domain and range restrictions. I did not want to give students very specific instructions because I felt that doing so would limit their creativity. Students had to use polynomial and rational functions but could also use any other functions they knew. I did not request a specific number of equations because I didn't want that to be the main factor driving their creativity and efforts. When students started to submit their work, I was truly amazed. Many students had used over thirty equations on their very first Desmos project. Here is a sample from our Horace Greeley math art:

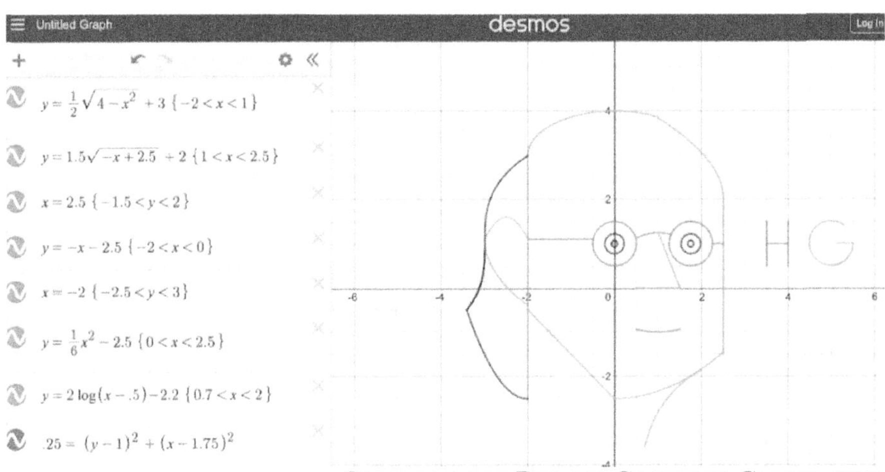

CREATED WITH DESMOS GRAPHING CALCULATOR

While students were working on their projects there was so much collaboration happening everywhere. I learned so many things about *Desmos* myself that I did not know prior to the project from my students. We spent two classes working on this activity. Many students were able to finish the entire project by the end of the second class while others continued to work at home. There was a strong sense of community and collaboration among students while working on this project. It was a total success, to the point that students requested two more *Desmos* art projects later on.

Last year, after our unit on conic sections, I gave the students a *Desmos* art project themed on Disney's *Encanto*. The projects consisted of recreating characters, covers, or scenes from the movie. Once again, the level of engagement was incredible. Each student picked what they wanted to recreate, and their passion came across in all the equations they created. Students found it very helpful to first upload the picture to *Desmos*, setting it as a background. They then proceeded to write all of their equations involving many of the units we had learned: polynomial, rational, conics, exponential, and logarithmic. Students do not need to have a *Desmos* account (although it may be helpful to have one) to be able to complete these projects. However, it is highly recommended that they save the link to their work. Here are a few samples of the amazing work my students completed this year:

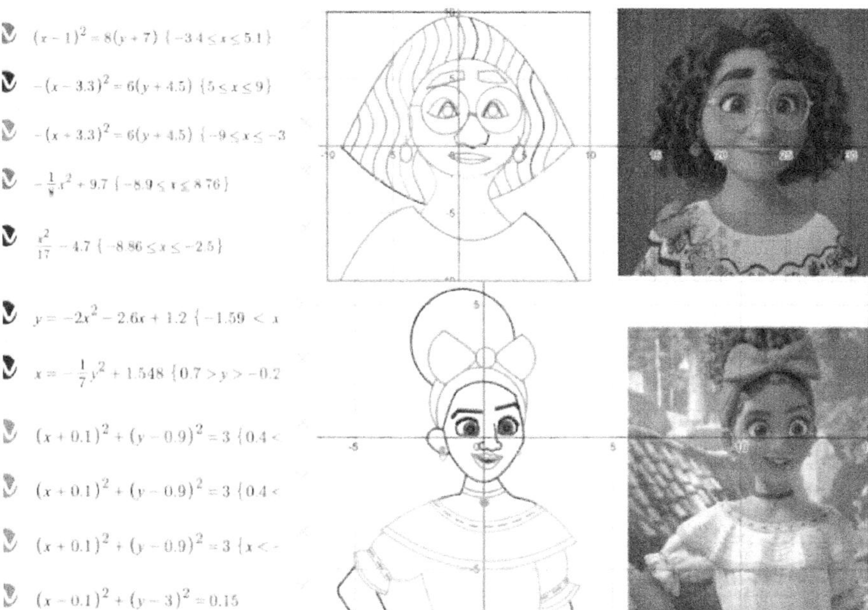

CREATED WITH DESMOS GRAPHING CALCULATOR

Similar to the previous year, we used a couple of classes to work on it and for many students this was the very first time they had used *Desmos*. I was really amazed by students' creativity and their tremendous effort. Truth be told, the quality of their work surpassed any expectation I had. Some students had over one hundred equations on their project which was not required in any way. It was also very interesting to witness how they thought about different types of functions that would best fit what they were trying to graph. There were rich math conversations happening inside and outside the classroom. Within the context of MathPlay, my students were able to apply rigorous math concepts and collaborate with one another. We need to provide our students with more opportunities like this.

I really hope you consider using a *Desmos* art project at some point. The project can be tailored to whatever math class you're currently teaching and it's a fantastic opportunity to give your students voice and choice in how they can demonstrate mastery of their learning. To give you an idea or starting point, here is a sample of the instructions I used for one of the *Desmos* art projects:

Desmos Art Project: Your assignment is to create Desmos art about a topic you are passionate about. Your project should include at least eight different types of functions: linear, quadratic, exponential, trigonometric, logarithmic, etc. You are not limited to the number of equations you use. Feel free to make any domain/range restrictions for your project. You can also use any other functions you have learned in the past.

You will submit:

- The original picture
- Desmos Link
- Screenshot of Desmos project including equations
- You will be graded (10 points possible) on:
- Use of at least eight different types of functions (4 points)
- Submitted original picture (2 points)
- Submitted Desmos link (2 points)
- Submitted screenshot of project with equations (2 points)

MATHPLAY VIA ANCHOR CHARTS

I recently started using anchor charts which I (wrongly) assumed were more of an idea for elementary students. An anchor chart is like a poster that can summarize important information or key points about a topic that can be retrieved later on. Having anchor charts around the classroom can be very helpful so that students have a resource to recall information other than the teacher. Using an anchor chart is definitely an awesome idea that can be very effective at all levels. I learned that providing students with an anchor chart can be very beneficial and it can sort of free the teacher from providing individual assistance with that specific topic. I noticed that when creating anchor charts with a class, I get to see what misconceptions students have and what topics they feel comfortable about.

I have also used anchor charts as a tool to facilitate MathPlay by having students create their own anchor charts with information they consider relevant or important. My daughter has also created some anchor charts on her own. I gave her a topic (in this case we were talking about shapes) and then I told her to make a chart with all the information she remembered about that shape. It was really interesting to see what she remembered and the connections she was making. Here are a couple of samples from the ones she made:

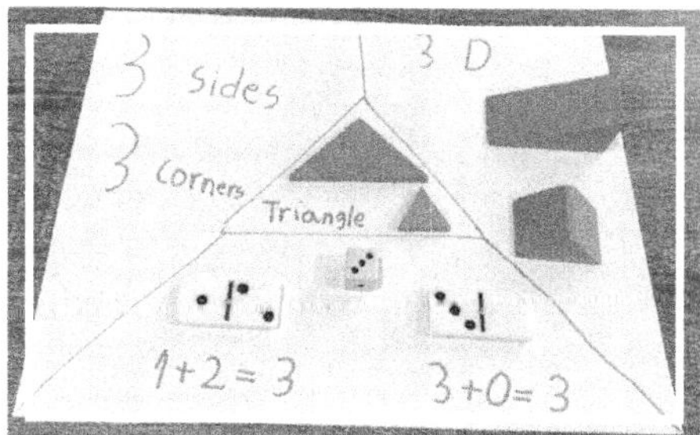

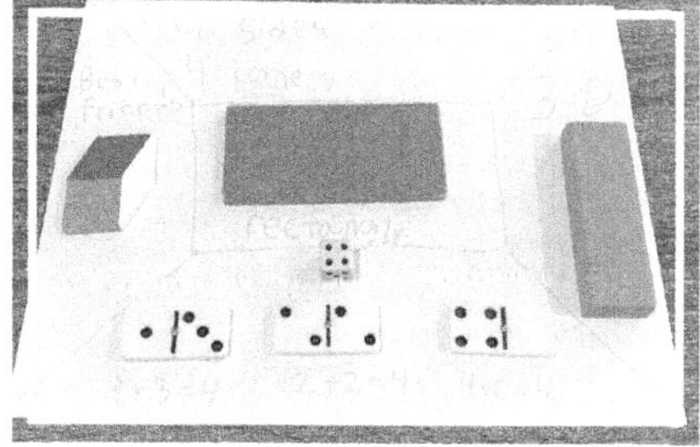

I particularly loved the "Best Friends" section on the rectangle anchor chart. It was an authentic perspective from a young learner. She felt that it was relevant to include the rectangle's best friends: square and rhombus. This was the last section she completed. It wasn't a formal mathematical concept but it gave her a sense of ownership over the chart. After the rectangle, she decided she was going to make another chart where she was going to add two dimensional shapes to create a three dimensional shape.

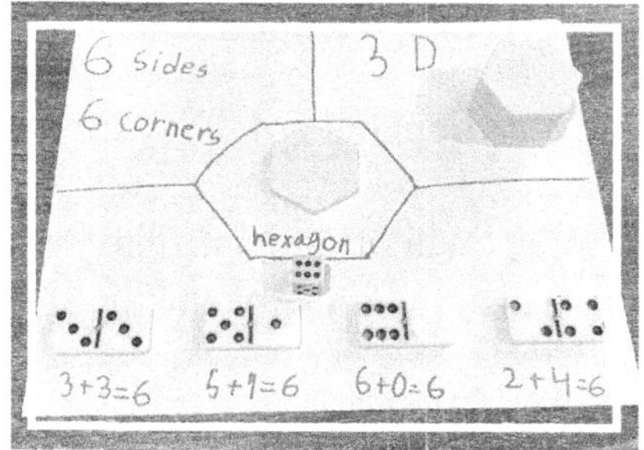

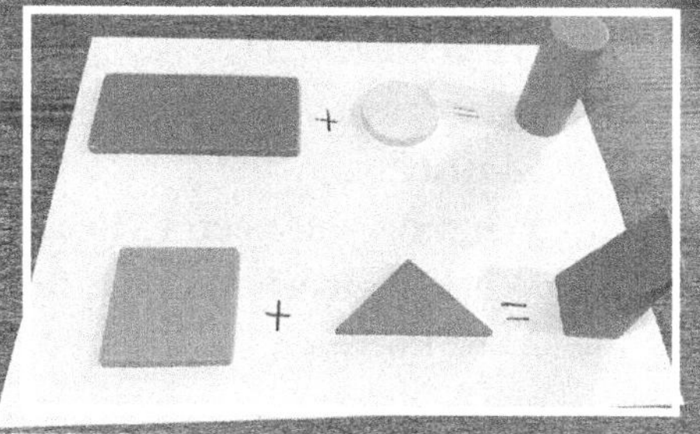

Seeing her make her own anchor charts was a lot of fun. With my high school students, we have made anchor charts as a class summarizing the key concepts or ideas of a lesson. The example on the left shows an anchor chart we created together about simplifying radicals. Just like at home, I would ask students to make their own anchor charts at the end of a lesson or towards the end of a unit. I thought this would be a good strategy to consolidate what they had learned while at the same time creating a helpful resource in preparation for a future assessment.

Here are a couple of samples from algebra and precalculus students within the units of radicals and sequences/series. I now know that anchor charts can be very useful both for elementary and secondary students.

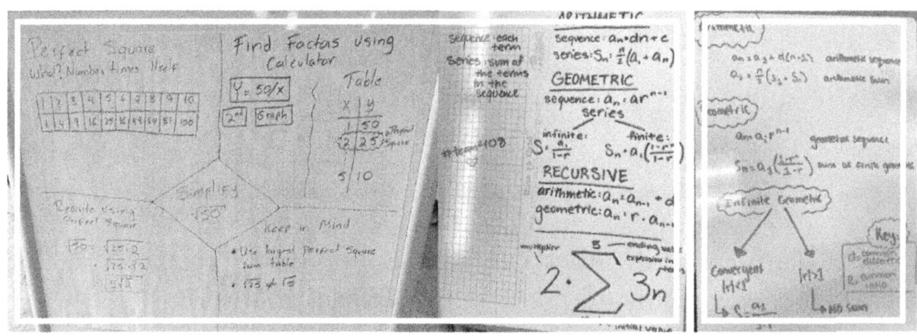

I hope that at this point, you are already thinking about specific topics and ideas to embed MathPlay to the lessons you have. We will now explore some tech tools that can help you facilitate MathPlay in the classroom or at home.

REFLECTION QUESTIONS

1. What are some student/teacher benefits of facilitating MathPlay?
2. What do you need to be able to start facilitating MathPlay?
3. What concerns come to mind with the idea of facilitating MathPlay?

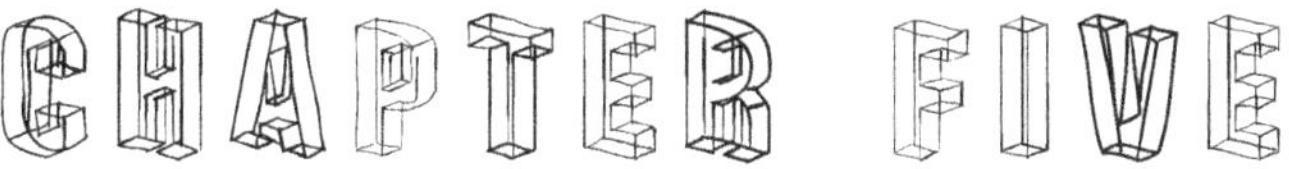

CHAPTER FIVE

TECHNOLOGY PROVIDES A POWERFUL WAY TO ENGAGE STUDENTS, INFORM INDIVIDUAL AND GROUP INSTRUCTION, DIFFERENTIATE LESSONS, DOCUMENT WORK, AND EMPOWER STUDENTS TO DIRECT THEIR OWN LEARNING.

STACEY ROSHAN

TECH TOOLS THAT HELP FACILITATE MATHPLAY

AS A STUDENT IN any class, I always enjoyed whenever we got to use a tech tool during a lesson or for a particular assignment. Even if it was something small like using the graphing calculator or a particular website, I found the use of technology to be very engaging from my perspective as a student. Educators worldwide are constantly learning and using different technologies in schools. From their school LMS (Learning Management System) to specific classroom tools, we are constantly updating our tech knowledge. It's likely that there is at least one tech tool you're using this school year that you did not use in previous years.

I firmly believe that we, as educators, do way more than just teach content. Can you think of a time you checked on a student after noticing they were acting differently? Our students are not machines or blank slates. Effective teaching requires making a human connection that is beneficial for both teachers and students. For that reason, I've never considered that technology will eventually replace what teachers do in a classroom. I understand that we all have different levels of comfort with technology and that's okay. However, technological advances will inevitably have a direct impact in how we continue to teach and learn for as long as we are in the profession.

During the 2019-2020 school year, we all had to face the reality of a global pandemic. Many teachers worldwide, myself included, left school one day and were told to bring home whatever they needed to be able to teach their classes remotely. This was definitely a historic time in education that had a significant impact in how technology is being utilized in schools today. There were many versions of remote learning at the time, some synchronous and some asynchronous. However, there was a common trend within all versions; teachers found themselves implementing new technologies to be able to reach their students. Within days, many teachers were making video lessons, facilitating live virtual lessons, grading work online, and using multiple online tools to engage students in learning; tools they'd only just learned to use.

Despite the overwhelming and unprecedented circumstances we were all facing, we did our best to reach and support our students using the technology we had available. I'm not suggesting in any way that using technology made it the same as teaching in person. I often share that whenever I was teaching online, I felt like a lion in a cage. Whenever I was teaching online, I felt very limited in my ability to interact with students. However, teaching them online was better than not being able to teach them at all.

During this time, in an effort to actively engage students, I tried many different tech tools and platforms. Some of these tools I was really learning and exploring myself, but I knew that using them with my students could make a difference in how they engaged with the content. As the months went by, my school transitioned from an online model (100% students remote) to a hybrid model (students online and in-person), to finally a back in person model. Many of the tools I used were effective in all the models we experienced and I'm still using them today. Given everything that was happening and considering that most educators had very little to no experience teaching remotely, I now feel it was an appropriate time to try new things in the classroom.

I learned that it was possible to leverage technology in the classroom to facilitate MathPlay regardless of the teaching model being used (remote, hybrid, or in-person). I'd like to share about my experience using four specific tools that I found effective with my students at school and also with my daughter at home.

MATH LEARNING CENTER (MLC)

I first learned about *MLC* via Twitter. As a teacher, I wasn't familiar with *MLC*, likely because my teaching experience has been at the high school and college levels. I noticed a few posts of young children working with very interactive and engaging tools which sparked my curiosity. Directly from the *MLC* website:

"The Math Learning Center (MLC) is a nonprofit organization serving the education community. Our mission is to inspire and enable individuals to discover and develop their mathematical confidence and ability. We offer innovative and standards-based curriculum, resources, and professional development. Our products and services are used by educators throughout the United States and in many international locations."

I knew this was definitely a resource I could use with my daughter at home. As I started exploring *MLC*, I came across their free apps which I would highly recommend for any elementary students and educators.

As I mentioned before, at home, we have different sets and games that we use anytime we're MathPlay-ing. We noticed that in one of the free apps, *Pattern Shapes*, the virtual shapes matched one of the sets we had at home. Many times, Mariana builds a pattern or a picture on the app and then recreates it using her shapes set.

This has become a very engaging activity for her. I particularly like how she's able to rotate different shapes sometimes for the purpose of being more symmetric and sometimes just because she's having fun.

One day while we were exploring, she suggested we check out *Geoboard* from *MLC*. She had used geoboards both in school and at home. She ended up doing something similar where she created some math art on the virtual geoboard and then recreated it with her shapes set. Any time we use *MLC* apps, my daughter is very engaged, open to explore, and MathPlay.

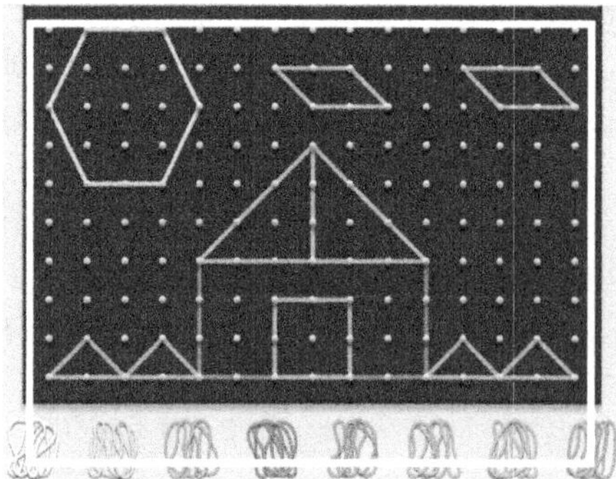

Recently, my daughter was learning how to tell time on an analog clock in the context of first grade. We used *Math Clock* from *MLC* as a resource. I love how the app provides different scaffolds as students are getting more familiarized in how to read time on a clock. We found this app very helpful as it provided unlimited opportunities for practice within different settings.

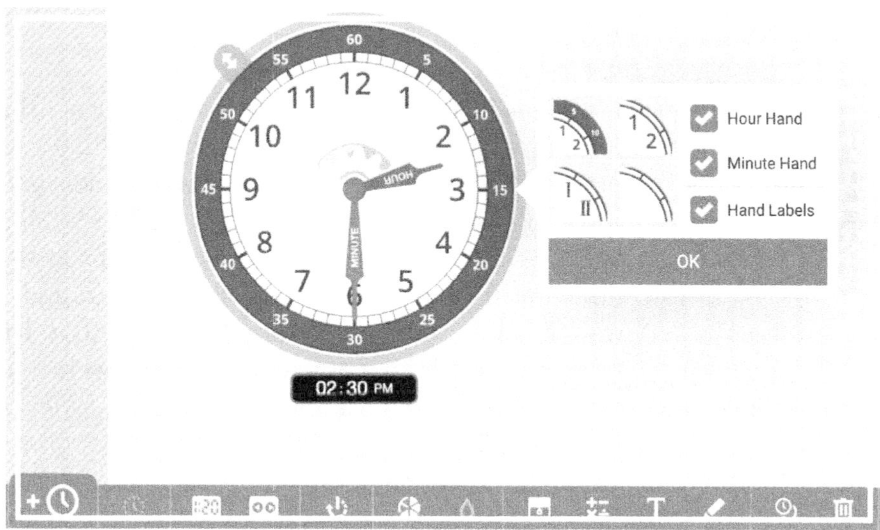

Another very cool feature of *MLC* is that during special holidays or dates, they provide activities for elementary students of different grade levels that are related to the holiday being celebrated. The activities sometimes involve shape patterns or different arithmetic operations. This is an example of an activity we completed centered on Valentine's Day:

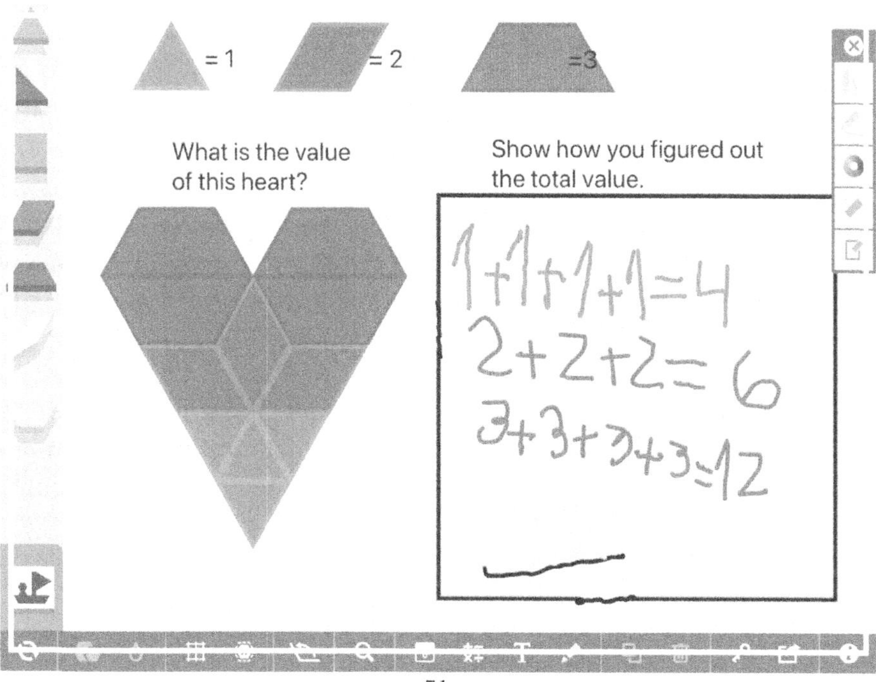

GRASPABLE MATH

I first learned about *Graspable Math* at the beginning of the pandemic back in 2020. As many other teachers, I was looking for tools and ways to help support my students while teaching them remotely. I was making video lessons at the time, and I remember specifically trying to find a way for my students to practice how to solve linear equations step-by-step. I felt that my video lessons were not enough since students were not able to ask me live questions as there was less interaction in the remote setting.

I was well aware students were able to solve many questions online just within a few clicks. I felt we had the technology we needed but maybe it wasn't being used effectively. That's when I came across *Graspable Math.* I was really impressed by how interactive and user-friendly the site was. I also enjoyed reading about the vision the designers had in mind when *Graspable Math* was developed. If you visit the website and click on the "About" session you can learn about their story. Here is an excerpt that resonated with me:

"In a world where technology has advanced at astonishing rates, the technology of math notation hasn't really changed in 400 years. The easiest way to write and solve an equation is still by hand, on paper. For a few years, a group of us—math educators, psychologists, mathematicians, and computer scientists—have been imagining ways to reconstruct the idea of formal notation by using digital technology. We think it's time to apply modern design approaches to build more intuitive and fluid interfaces for math. We want tools that scaffold experiences of algebraic structure, supports genuine inquiry about how math works, and gives people opportunities to reason flexibly about mathematics."

Within their math whiteboard, *Graspable Math* allows students to type in an equation they want to solve. They can then drag terms from one side of the equation to the other, while doing so, students will notice the sign of that term will change.

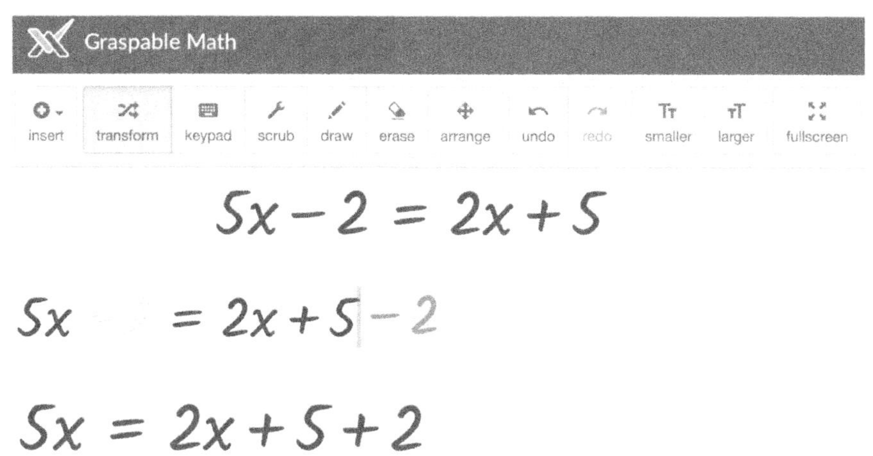

Students can then combine like terms by dragging and dropping. Graspable Math ensures that this only works for actual like terms.

$$5x = 2x + 5 + 2$$

$$5x = 2x + 7$$

$$5x - 2x = 7$$

$$3x = 7$$

At this point in the example, students need to divide by 3 to be able to solve for x. As students grab the 3 from the left side to bring it to the right side, they will notice that it goes from multiplication to division.

$$x = \frac{7}{3}$$

$$x = \frac{7}{3}$$

Once students are done with solving the equation, *Graspable Math* provides an amazing feature where students are able to see all of their digital work in a step-by-step sequence. There are a couple of circles next to the equation that can be expanded by scrolling down.

$$5x - 2 = 2x + 5$$

$$5x = 2x + 5 + 2$$

$$5x = 2x + 7$$

$$5x - 2x = 7$$

$$3x = 7$$

$$x = \frac{7}{3}$$

As a mathematics educator and learner, I think of *Graspable Math* as a safe math "playground" where students are able to practice their skills while exploring mathematical ideas. I also find the platform to be very inviting for students. There is something very powerful and engaging in being able to manipulate the terms of an equation while solving it. Since students are using virtual manipulatives, there is an emphasis in the process of how to arrive at the solution instead of just finding it.

This is only a sample but there is a lot more you can do if you go on to explore *Graspable Math* by yourself.

I find the platform to be very useful whenever I'm working with individual students or small groups. Students seem to enjoy using *Graspable Math* as it feels like they're playing a game where they win by following the "math" rules. I have also used it with my daughter as we practice her addition and subtraction skills. The use of virtual manipulatives comes very natural to children, especially in the context of safe MathPlay.

DESMOS

Over recent years, as for many other math teachers, *Desmos* has become an integral tool in my instruction. Whether it's for the purpose of exploration or the delivery of content, I find myself regularly using *Desmos* with my students regardless of the class or level being taught. I believe that most math teachers would share the vision of *Desmos Studio* about mathematics and education.

"Desmos Studio is a Public Benefit Corporation with a goal of helping everyone learn math, love math, and grow with math. We believe that everyone is an inner mathematician and that some people haven't been given the opportunity, encouragement, or tools to discover theirs. So we prioritize equity and accessibility at every level of our work."

You can learn more about *Desmos* (Studio & Classroom) and what they do by visiting their site and clicking on the "About Us" section.

I started using and recommending the free *Desmos* graphing calculator years back. It was particularly helpful for students who did not have their own graphing calculator at home. Nowadays, I'm using the platform for so much more than just graphing. I regularly use it to run my lessons and facilitate student exploration in what feels like a very safe and interactive environment. It's also worth mentioning that I've used it while teaching in person, remotely, and also in a hybrid model.

As a mathematics educator and learner, I think *Desmos Classroom* does an amazing job with its activities. They are highly interactive and user friendly. I particularly love how the activities help facilitate exploration of rich mathematical concepts in a natural way. If you haven't checked them out yet, I strongly encourage you to do so by scanning the QR code.

There are four specific free *Desmos Classroom* activities I've found very useful when facilitating MathPlay. In *Land the Plane,* students use their knowledge of the equation of a line to provide a safe path of landing for a virtual airplane. This is an extremely engaging lesson that can be edited or adjusted to meet the needs of different learners. I usually start the lesson with a check in and then a quick review of slope-intercept form. As soon as students start landing planes, it really feels like they are playing a game.

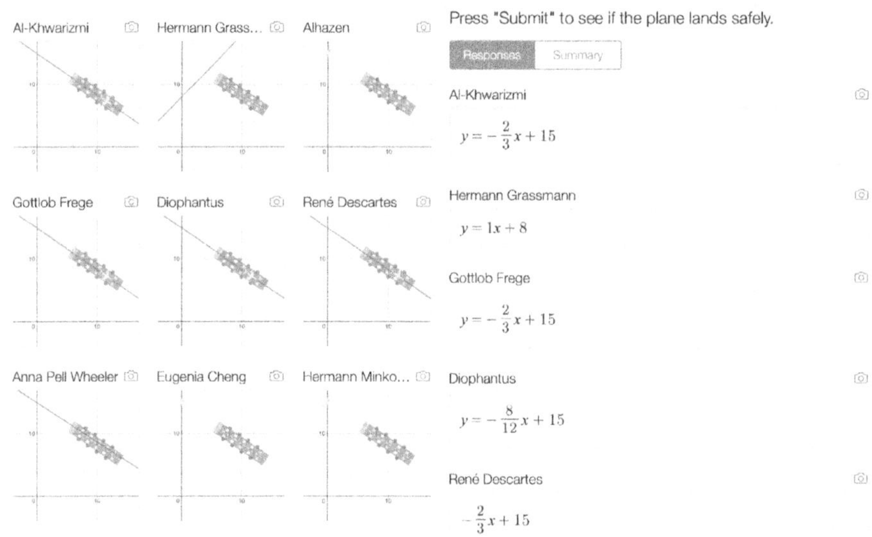

Screenshots of freely-available Desmos activities are used with permission from Amplify Education, Inc.

Students have always provided very positive feedback about the *Land the Plane* lesson. It's also an activity they seem to remember. When I've run into former students, many of them remember the day we landed planes using math.

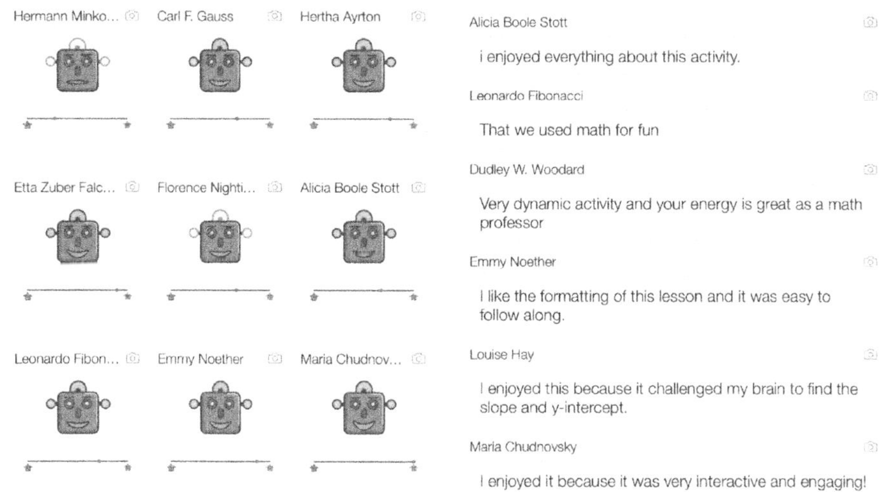

DESMOS GIVES THE OPTION TO ANONYMIZE STUDENTS BY GIVING THEM NAMES OF FAMOUS MATHEMATICIANS

Another awesome *Desmos* activity is *Marbleslides: Exponentials* (there are other *Marbleslides* activities for different types of functions) in which the goal is for students to hit all the stars by applying transformations to different exponential functions. My students have found this activity extremely engaging due to it's game-based nature. Similar to *Land the Plane*, it can be adjusted to the needs of various learners.

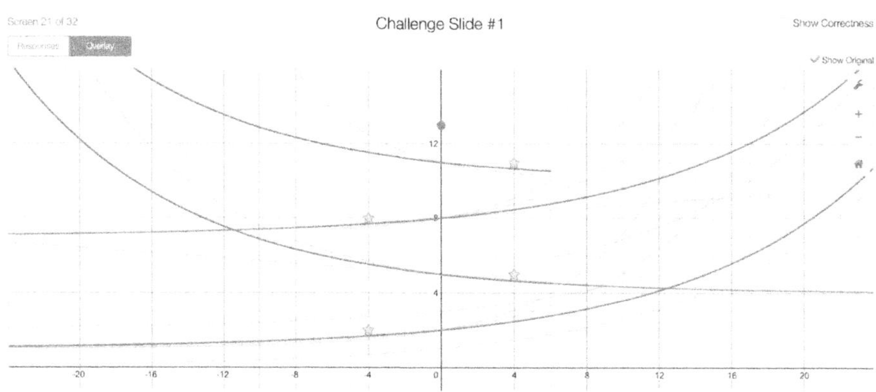

In *Pool Border Problem* students need to figure out how many blocks are required to go around a pool of different sizes. They must first use numeric solutions that then scaffold to a general solution in the form of an expression. Students have multiple attempts and the program does a great job in helping students make their thinking visible.

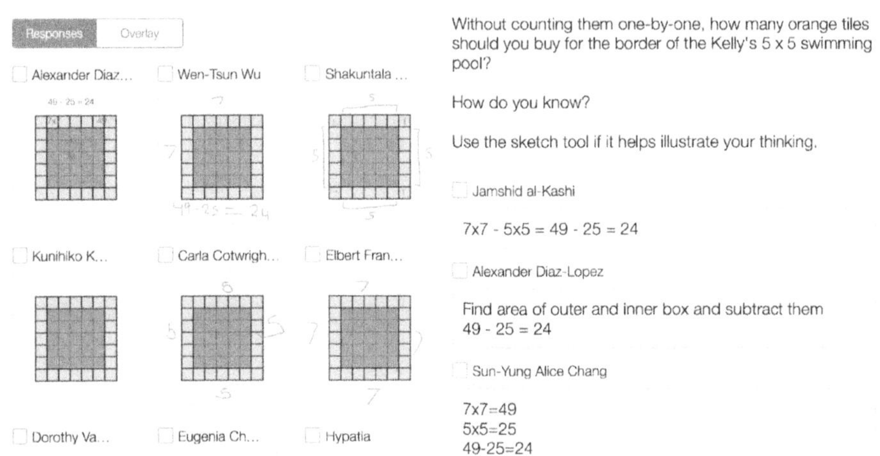

I love how in this lesson there is a natural transition in the solution from specific numeric to a more general expression. It's also interesting as a teacher to see how students type in their expressions in different formats. It's like looking into their thinking by analyzing how they decided to approach the problem.

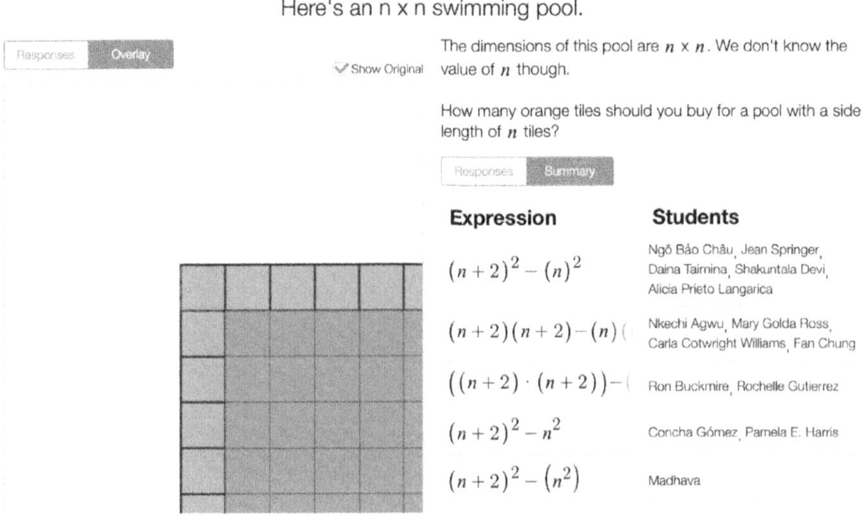

Finally, *Balloon Float* is one of my favorites. It also provides a very engaging way to explore ratios and proportions. In this activity students determine how many balloons are needed for different objects to float in the air.

One Balloon

It took 4 balloons to make the duck float. The duck weighs 56 grams.

With 1 balloon, how many grams could you make float?

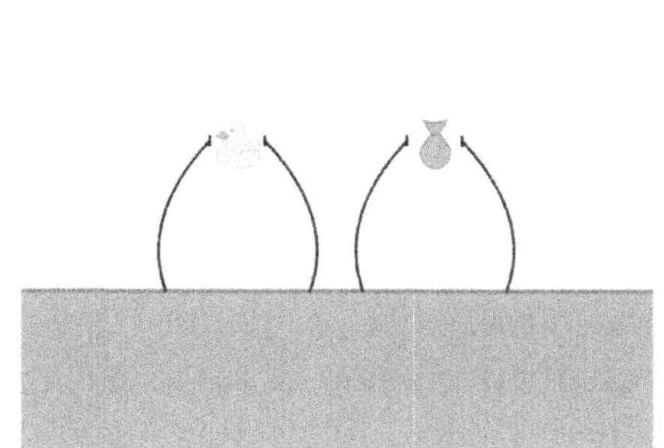

All of these activities and many more are currently available for free at the *Desmos Classroom* site all of which are extremely interactive.

As of June 2022, *Desmos Tools* (i.e., all *Desmos* calculators) became a part of a new independent public benefit corporation called *Desmos Studio PBC*. *Desmos Classroom*, which includes the *Desmos* Activity Builder and ready-made *Desmos* Activities cited in this book, is now owned, and managed by Amplify Education, Inc. The *Desmos Classroom* platform remains free for users worldwide.

GEOGEBRA

I first learned about *GeoGebra* in grad school while I was enrolled in a class called Exploring Mathematics Using Technology back in the Fall of 2013. In class, I remember using *GeoGebra* mostly as a graphing tool while exploring properties of different functions as well as in the context of visualizing concepts in geometry. Once I started teaching, I would recommend *GeoGebra* to students who did not have a graphing calculator at home. However, the platform does so much more than graph. Directly from the site:

"GeoGebra is a dynamic mathematics software for all levels of education that brings together geometry, algebra, spreadsheets, graphing, statistics, and calculus in one engine. In addition, GeoGebra offers an online platform with over 1 million free classroom resources created by our multilingual community. These resources can be easily shared through our collaboration platform GeoGebra Classroom where student progress can be monitored in real time."

I have used *GeoGebra* with my students both in person and remote to facilitate MathPlay. One activity my geometry students really enjoy is taking a picture of something that looks like a parallelogram, uploading it, and then proving whether or not it is in fact a parallelogram using a method of their choice. Once the image is uploaded to *GeoGebra*, students can use all the tools available to perform computations and double check their work.

Students have completed this activity both remotely and in-person where they took a picture of an object around their house or our school. In the example below, using the coordinates in *GeoGebra,* this student used the midpoint formula to show that the diagonals of the shape bisected each other, therefore proving that it was a parallelogram.

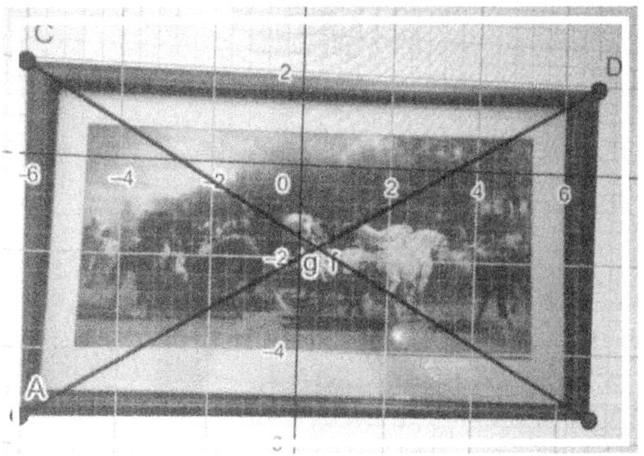

I always ask students to submit a picture of the shape they've uploaded as well as their work or an explanation. This is an activity I would highly recommend for any geometry class. It really informs my teaching when I am able to see how students take different paths to prove or disprove that their shape is a parallelogram or not. The tools within *GeoGebra* are very intuitive which fosters further exploration.

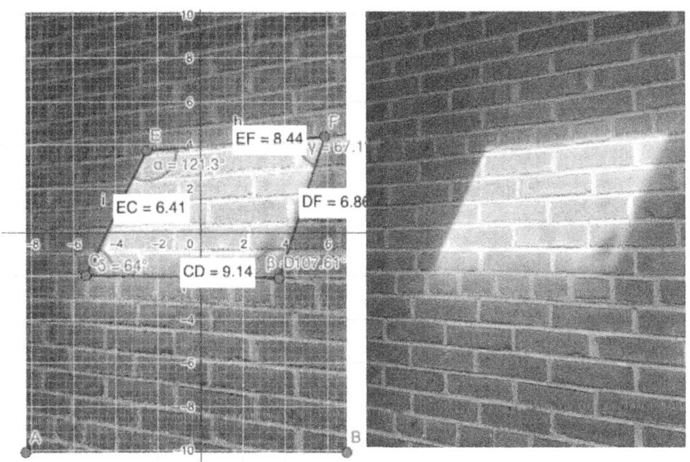

This is not a parallelogram because CD is not equal to EF, and DF is not equal to EC. Parallelograms have equal opposite sides, so this cannot be one. Along with this, their angles differ. Angle C is not the same as angle F, and angle E is not equal to angle D.

The platform has an animation feature that I find very powerful when exploring mathematical concepts. As an educator, I can explore so many more examples by simply adding a "slider" to a function. I recently started using this particular feature to make GIF (graphic interchange format) files for my students.

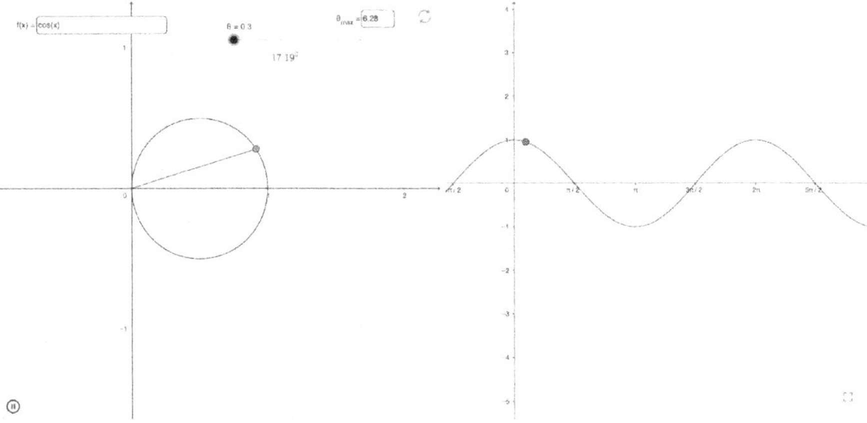

On one occasion, we were reviewing the graphs of sine and cosine and their relation to the unit circle. It's so powerful for students to see the relation of the cosine graph to the unit circle as the angle "slides" from 0 to 2π. I usually screen record the animation, save it as a GIF, and then share it with the class.

I've also used GIF files with my calculus students to help them visualize mathematical concepts. In the example below, students were able to see the tangent moving along the graph of sine and how as the points were plotted, the cosine function was graphed. Students will develop a deeper understanding by leveraging the technology we have available. I also would like to mention that I used this particular activity after attending a *GeoGebra* webinar facilitated by Steve Phelps who is always sharing his amazing resources via Twitter @MathTechCoach.

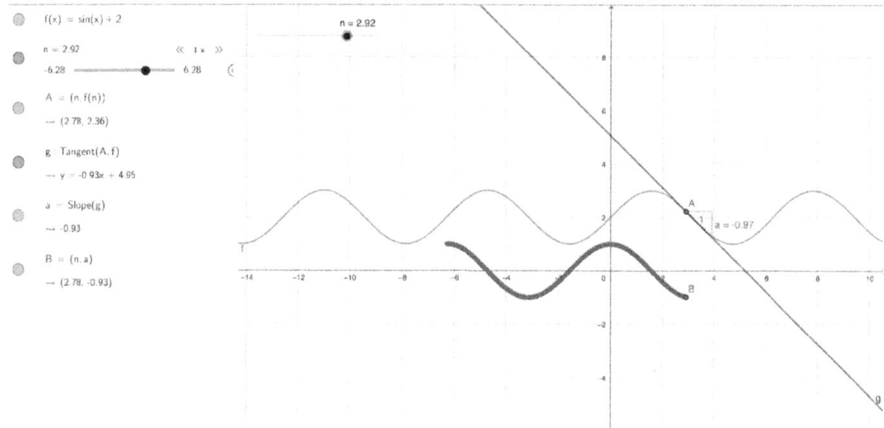

During the 2022 Florida *GeoGebra* conference, Rob Pontecorvo (@PotecorvoRob) did a wonderful presentation on using *GeoGebra* for gamification. Rob defined gamification as the process of adding games or game-like elements to something (such as a task) so as to encourage participation. *GeoGebra* is a fantastic interactive tool that can foster discovery-based learning.

I often find it very helpful to use MathPlay for students to practice a concept they have already learned in class. Whether it's for the purpose of independent or group practice, using MathPlay is really engaging for students. During his presentation, Rob shared a few applets that can be used to facilitate MathPlay. I particularly liked one he shared by Tim Brzezinski where students can have unlimited practice with interval notation. The applet includes single sets, conjunctions, and disjunctions.

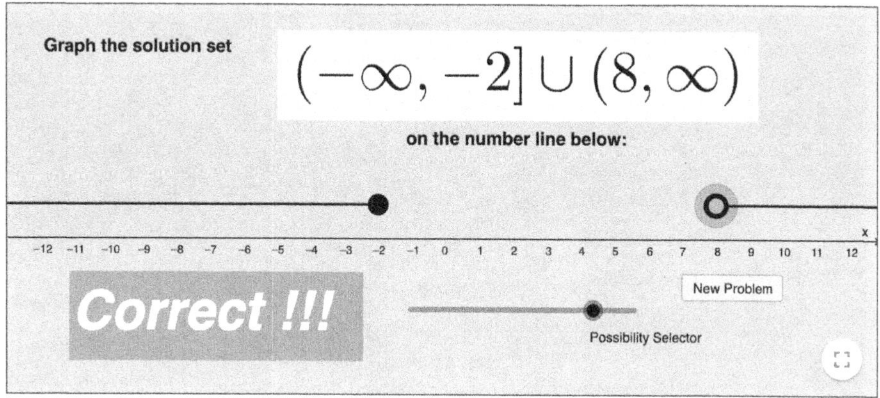

Students are given the solution set in interval notation and then have to graph the solution on a number line. Students move the "possibility selector" to choose the correct set-up then drag the circles to the correct endpoints. Once students have figured out the correct graph, the applet will give them feedback that their solution is accurate. Scan the QR code to explore the applet. Tim has pretty amazing resources he constantly shares via Twitter @TimBrzezinski.

If you teach younger students (or your own children), Rob also shared *Spaceship Race,* a game where students are able to practice addition and subtraction of integers. The player is given a question to answer with three choices. If answered correctly, the spaceship will move towards the finish line. The goal of course is to get to the finish line before your opponent. Scan the QR code to explore the applet.

When I started playing this game with my daughter, she wasn't a big fan as she would get nervous about making mistakes and losing the race. We started playing together, taking turns against the opponent which gave her confidence. Since she hasn't officially learned about negative numbers in first grade, she was sometimes confused if the answer was supposed to be negative but one of the choices was positive. I have really enjoyed watching her play this game, her mental math has definitely gotten stronger as a result.

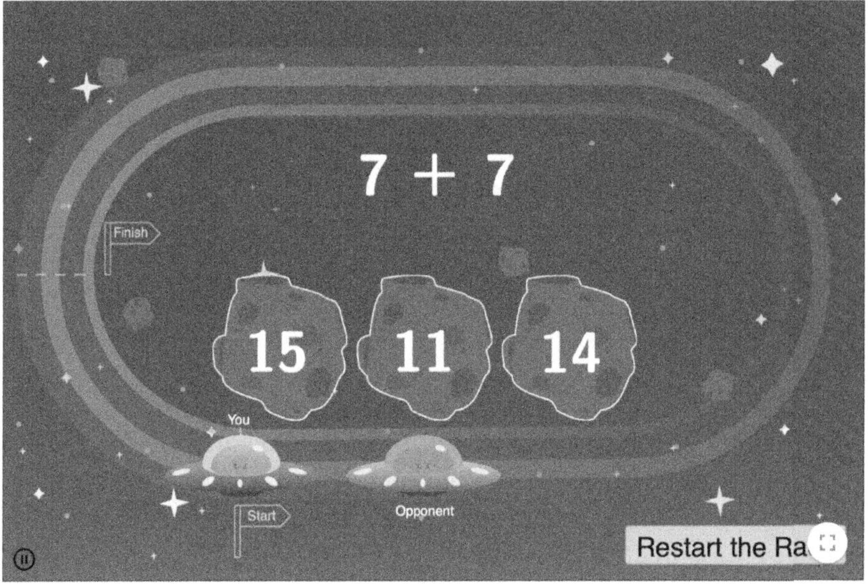

These activities are only a small sample of the many amazing resources you can find in *GeoGebra*.

REFLECTION QUESTIONS

1. What tech tools are you currently using with your students? How does it facilitate your instruction?
2. What tech tools would you like to explore or learn more about? What benefits would they have for you and/or your students?
3. Would it be possible to explore the tools with a colleague or group of colleagues? What would you need to get started?

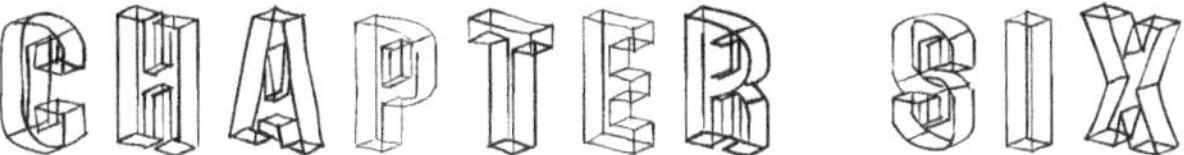

CHAPTER SIX

MATHEMATICS IS NOT ABOUT NUMBERS, EQUATIONS, COMPUTATIONS, OR ALGORITHMS; IT IS ABOUT UNDERSTANDING.

WILLIAM PAUL TURSTON

MORE RESOURCES FOR MATHPLAY

FACILITATING MATHPLAY WITH MY students does not always involve an activity that takes the entire class period or requires specific tech tools. Many times, we get to MathPlay at the very beginning of the lesson during our activation time. Whatever we do as teachers, the first five to ten minutes of class sets the tone for the rest of the lesson. Similarly, the way we end our lessons is also an opportunity to make connections, consolidate, and MathPlay.

Truth be told, for a long time the beginning of my lessons was very traditional and always the same. There was a "Do Now" question for students which usually required a skill from a previous lesson and/or a question that scaffolded a skill needed for that day. As a math student, this is how class started for me most of the time. Reviewing and scaffolding are very effective ways to start class, however, when I opened a Twitter account back in 2019, I learned about other activation routines that can also be very effective to start class. There are three activations that I really like as they facilitate welcoming math conversations that feel like MathPlay. *Which One Doesn't Belong*, *Same but Different*, and *Visual Patterns* are probably the ones I use the most across the classes I teach and with my daughter at home.

These activations can lead to authentic conversations where students are not limited to only finding the "right" answer. There is a sense of wonder and exploration, which should be vital components in all math classes. The more engaged our students are, the deeper understanding they will get out of our lessons. Engaging our students can be challenging at times; think about all the different apps and content they have available at their fingertips.

One thing my students love are memes. They are very popular in social media and we're constantly getting new ones. Memes can be very useful in math class for different purposes. I learned that just like students enjoy them on social media, they also enjoy them in math class. Using different activations and memes in class has contributed to a positive and playful classroom culture where students are more willing to share without worrying about being right or wrong. I'd like to share about my experiences with each routine and also from some of the educators that came up with some innovative ideas.

MATH MEMES

As mentioned, math memes can be used in different ways and for different purposes. I have used them at the beginning or the end of a lesson to emphasize an important concept or idea. I have also used them during a lesson to make connections with other topics. Regardless of when in the lesson you use them, one common trend is that understanding a math meme requires understanding the math it references. In a way, I like to think about math memes as applied mathematics. It's also not too hard to find math memes on almost any topic you're teaching with a quick Google search.

Some of the most creative memes I've seen did not come directly from a Google search however, they came from Fresno State professor Howie Hua, who teaches math to future elementary school teachers. Luckily for all of us, Howie is always sharing tips, memes, and explainer videos via TikTok and Twitter @howie_hua. I reached out to Howie to find out more about his rationale and inspiration for his math memes and this was his response:

"Sharing memes is one of my love languages so I think sharing math memes that I've made makes me happy. Laughter is one of the greatest gifts and to hear people laughing because of my memes makes my day. For the past couple of years, I end every class session with a "Meme of the Day" that I've created just so the class session ends with a laugh (and even if it's not a laugh, they can see that I tried). At

the end of the course, I give an optional assignment for students to make a meme of me/the course and those are always great - a lot of wholesome ones, too!"

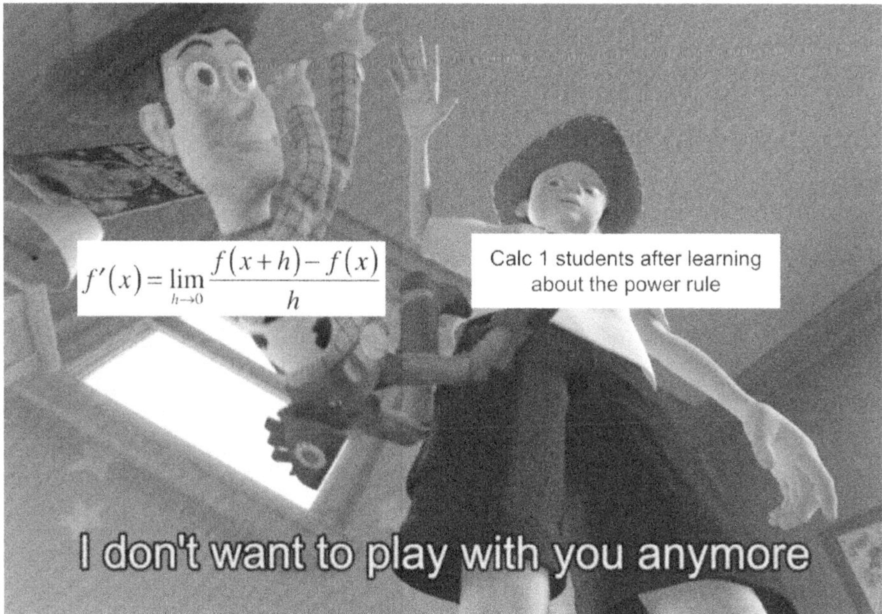

These are two great examples of Howie's creativity. You can find a full collection of memes by scanning the QR code.

During the 2020-2021 school year, I had a

geometry class full of students who loved *Star Wars*. They were so eager to talk about *Star Wars* and share their expertise. As you can guess, I started looking for *Star Wars* math memes.

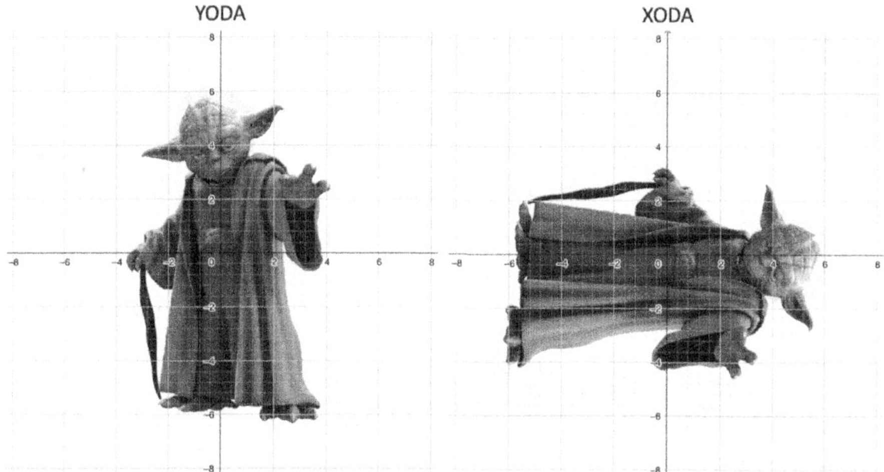

Courtesy of Twitter Account @StarWarsMath

Using math memes of shows my students watch has been a very effective way to connect with them beyond the classroom. As Howie mentioned, even if they don't find it funny, they see that I tried. I've gotten emails from students of memes they have found, referencing something we learned in class. Another awesome Twitter account dedicated to memes is @memecrashes.

SAME BUT DIFFERENT MATH

I first learned about *Same But Different Math* while attending a webinar facilitated by Dr. Sue Looney. I was immediately hooked. It felt to me like such a natural routine that can be used to understand both simple and complex concepts. I reached out to Dr. Looney to learn about the rationale and inspiration behind her awesome idea. Here is what she had to share:

WHY SAME BUT DIFFERENT MATH?

What is one of the first things you do when you encounter something new? What happens cognitively when you find yourself in a novel situation or location or presented with new information? You assimilate that new information into your already existing knowledge. You've been doing that your whole life–from birth onwards. Think about a baby who cries when handed to a stranger. What is happening there? Among many things, this new and different person lacks familiarity and connection to all that the baby knows. Think about stepping off of an airplane after traveling to a foreign country. All of your senses are immediately engaged in the "newness" of language, sights, smells, etc. Now, think about encountering fractions for the first time. Or percents. Or solid shapes. What feelings does this evoke for you? What is your initial reaction? And then what happens?

In all of these scenarios, you are involved in sense-making as you gain more and more knowledge and life experiences. One of the most natural things you do as you begin this sense-making journey is to compare and search for connections. What is the same about this new thing? But also, what is different? How is this new experience or piece of information connected to what you know to be true and yet how is this uniquely different?

The number sense routine of Same But Different Math harnesses the power of what we do naturally as we learn by playfully connecting mathematical concepts. In using this routine with students, students are engaged and empowered by having agency over their learning. Using this routine, students are able to build bridges and connections between existing math knowledge and new ideas. Additionally, they are able to fill in their understanding of previously learned concepts to develop a more robust understanding with connections. Whether participants are young preschoolers or adult learners, all learners benefit from explicitly comparing and contrasting mathematical ideas.

SAME BUT DIFFERENT MATH IN ACTION

Let's take a look at preschoolers making sense of an early numeracy concept using the Same But Different Math number sense routine.

When students are developing their cardinal understanding of numbers–that is when they understand that the counting process tells them how many they have of something–they can be surprised that two different sets of objects that look different can have the same numerosity. They are working through the idea that two sets of three, for example, can be the Same But Different.

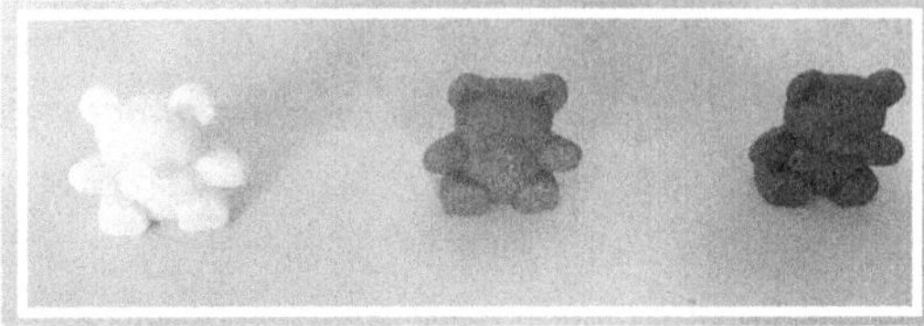

WWW.SAMEBUTDIFFERENTMATH.COM/EARLY-NUMERACY

Using this image above, students are asked to look at the image and think how they would finish the following sentences:

They are the same because ________________________.
They are different because ________________________.

After thinking silently, students have an opportunity to turn and talk to a partner, followed by a whole class sharing. Here are some of the comments from some four-year olds. As you read them, consider this: What do you learn about their mathematical understanding and knowledge from each of their comments below?

"They are the same because they both show bears."

"There's a yellow and a yellow, and a green and a green and a blue and a blue."

"One is bigger than the other one."

"One they are away from each other and the other they are near each other."

"I see one, two, three and one, two, three. They both show three."

Many important ideas surfaced in this discussion. Which attributes are present in this image? What kind of positional language can be used to describe the image? How much IS "one, two, three?" Is "one bigger than the other one" or do "they both show three?" By presenting students with an image designed to evoke conversations about counting, students are engaged in a playful low-risk activity while making sense of what they are seeing. At the same time, the teacher is able to assess for understanding, probe for explanation, and move students to deeper levels of making sense of counting.

Let's look in on an example from some older students using this image about an algebraic concept.

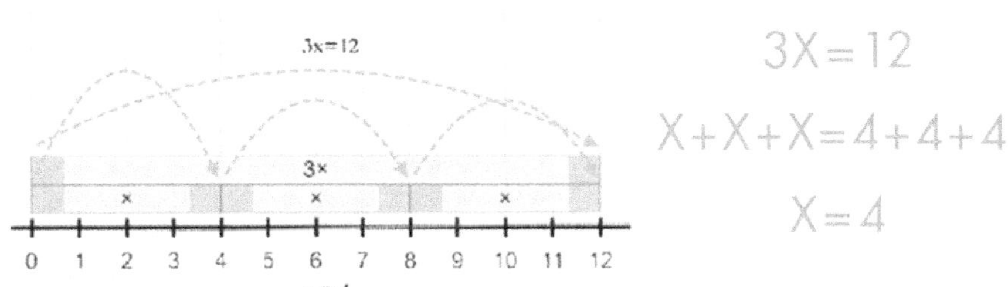

WWW.SAMEBUTDIFFERENTMATH.COM/ALGEBRA

Here we have two solutions to what is typically taught as solving a one-step equation for x. Rather than modeling the solution steps and asking students to then repeat those steps, the Same But Different Math routine can be used to help students consider other solution strategies as they connect to one another.

Here are some students comments after following the same protocol as described for the preschoolers (silently think, turn and talk, whole class share):

"Both show the solution to 3x=12 but they are solved in different ways."

"One is a number line and one is not."

"I don't get why neither of them just divided by 3?"

"I think that's shown by three jumps of x on the number line and then x + x + x in the other."

"One is a drawing and one is symbolic."

In this discussion as with the earlier example, we learn that students are making sense of many important ideas. What are variables? What does it mean to solve this equation? How does the number line model relate to the solution path? What are the connections between operations? We uncover that while a student might know the rule is to divide both sides by three, they may not understand what that means and why that is done.

Using the Same But Different Math routine, students are able to be observers, discoverers, sense-makers, and contributors to developing deeper understanding of mathematical ideas. There are endless opportunities to ask our students what is the same but different, leveraging this natural learning process while having fun in the math classroom!

SAME BUT DIFFERENT MATH AT THE SECONDARY LEVEL

The idea of using the *Same But Different Math* routine to make connections in the math classroom really resonated with me. One of my goals as a teacher is for all my students to feel comfortable and to be able to contribute to class discussion. I learned that using the routine *Same But Different Math* at the beginning of class can help promote a safe and welcoming environment where students are more open to sharing their ideas. At the time, I found myself navigating the *Same But Different Math* site and finding multiple images I was able to use with my students. I was able to find examples from early numeracy to algebra and geometry. While using the routine with my students, I learned it can be very effective at the high school and even college levels.

I was teaching precalculus and calculus, so I started creating my own examples of *Same But Different Math* tailored to those specific subjects. Once you are comfortable using the routine, you will come up with your own ideas as there is plenty of comparing and contrasting in mathematics. Here are a couple of examples:

Activation: Same but Different

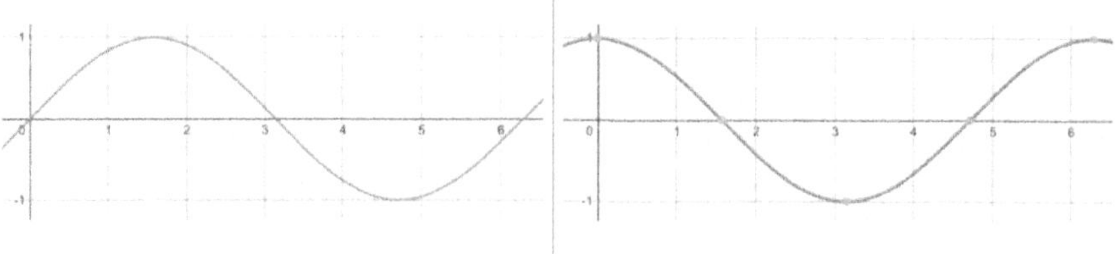

This example compares the graphs of the sine and cosine functions. I used it with my precalculus students as we were starting our unit of polar coordinates and needed to review graphs of trigonometric functions. The conversation was so rich, students had so much to share. For *Same* they mentioned amplitude, period, both trigonometric, both waves, max, and min. For *Different* they mentioned sine starts at zero, cosine starts at one, and different graph colors. The conversation was completely controlled by student input and we were able to review so many properties in a very natural way.

After experiencing how successful the routine was with my high school students, I decided to give it a try with my students at the college. My calculus students were also willing to share. The routine was very effective in making connections between various differentiation rules and when to use them. Here is an example:

Same but Different

$y = (\ln x)^4$	$y = \ln x^4$
$y = (\ln x)^4$	$y = \ln x^4$
$y' = 4(\ln x)^3 \cdot \frac{1}{x}$	$y = 4 \ln x$
$y' = \frac{4(\ln x)^3}{x}$	$y' = 4 \cdot \frac{1}{x} = \frac{4}{x}$

Whether it was at the high school or college level, using Same But Different sets the stage for multiple voices to be heard and avoids a single student (or group of students) dominating the conversation. All of the images I've used with my students can be found at the Same But Different Math site in the High School section.

Recently, I got the *Same But Different Math* student cards for my daughter who is heading into second grade this coming school year. When we use the set, I usually select 10 cards with some ideas I want her to think about. She then picks one card at a time and tells me how the images are the same but different. I really love that if she's not sure about the math concept, she shares other characteristics (i.e. color, position, size, etc). Using the routine and the cards has not only helped her explore math concepts but also helped her become a stronger analyzer/observer who pays more attention to detail.

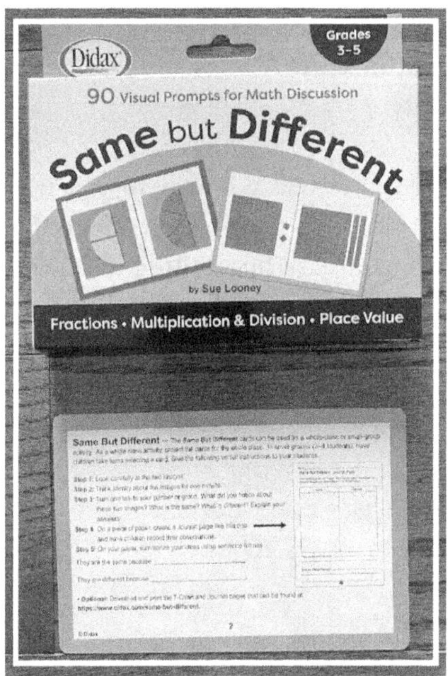

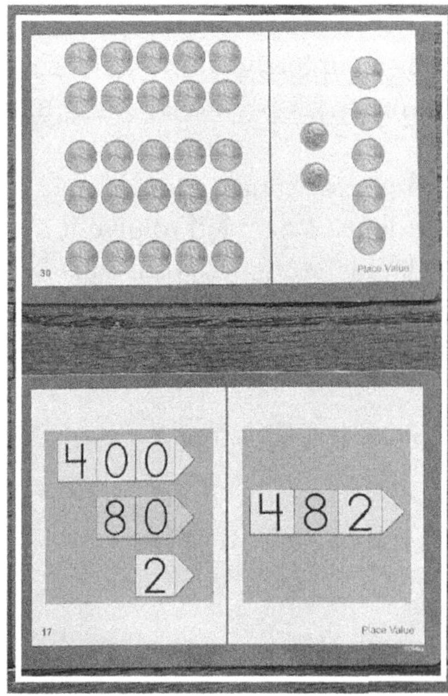

If you have little ones at home or if you teach them in school, I encourage you to check out the student card sets. There are two different sets for elementary levels - K-2 and 3-5.

VISUAL PATTERNS

During the pandemic when I was teaching remotely, I noticed students taking notes during our lessons. However, I felt as though they were not as engaged as I wanted them to be. They were more compliant than engaged. I remember some students asking questions via the private chat instead of speaking up. It was definitely a challenging time for all of us and I felt very limited in my ability to interact with students which is something that happens very naturally for me in an in-person class. I really wanted my students to feel comfortable enough to participate and ask questions in the remote environment.

One strategy that was extremely effective during this particular time was starting class with a visual pattern. I gave students a pattern and asked them to make or draw a prediction of the next step. After a few minutes, students will bring a drawing of their prediction closer to the camera all at the same time. Everyone was expected to share their prediction with the rest of the class. This ensured that everyone was actively participating and there was accountability. After we shared, there was a short follow up where students discussed some of their rationale for the next step and the conversations were awesome. I was very pleased to hear their discussions and happy with their willingness to share. Fawn Nguyen has done an amazing job organizing so many examples on her website. One of the first patterns I used with my students was pattern 109. Here is an example of the slide I gave students at the beginning of class and their predictions of step #4:

Patterns: Can you predict what #4 would look like?

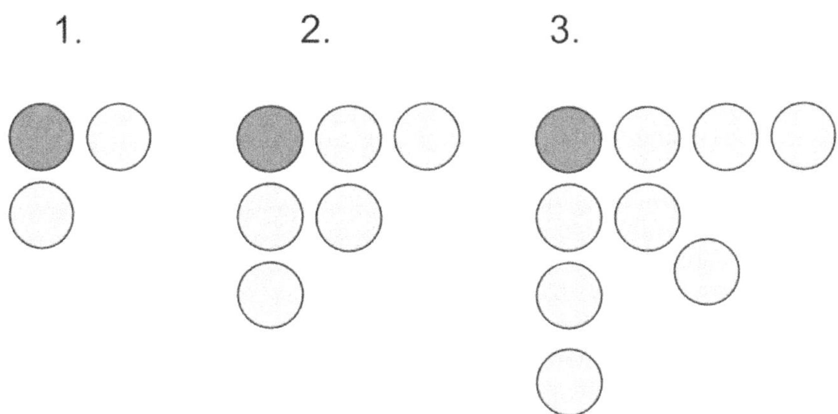

My students loved visual patterns and were really engaged in sharing how they went about their prediction. Any time we did a visual pattern, students were willing and open to discuss their ideas in a playful environment. As teachers, oftentimes we are able to recognize and capitalize on unexpected "teachable moments."

During the sharing out, sometimes there were disagreements which led to deeper mathematical conversations. Students naturally had to dig deeper to settle their disagreement. For example, they had to determine how many circles would be on a particular step. Or they had to come up with a formula that would help make a general prediction.

As I started using visual patterns more and more, I found that they could be extremely useful for many different topics with anyone who is learning math. I've used them at home with my daughter to count money or coins (one, five, ten, twenty-five) and also to explore shapes with different numbers of sides. At the high school level, using visual patterns has been an amazing resource for topics involving functions, polygons, sequences, series, etc.

My students and I have really enjoyed visual patterns. I decided to reach out to the mastermind behind the idea, Fawn Nguyen, to learn more about how the idea came about and how it has developed since then. Here are the questions I asked Fawn and what she had to share:

HOW DID THE IDEA COME ABOUT FOR YOU?

I took a summer math course at Portland State University (Oregon) back in the mid 90s. It was through the Math Learning Center which later created the elementary math curriculum, Bridges. That was my first formal exposure to visual patterns where we were given the first three stages of a pattern and asked to write an equation for it. I enjoyed the challenge and kept a notebook of the patterns I'd worked on. Fast forward to 2011 when I was teaching mathematics to middle schoolers, I created visualpatterns.org to share about 50 patterns I had at the time.

WHERE DO YOU FIND SOME OF YOUR INSPIRATION?

We have an affinity to seek patterns, and the classic definition of mathematics is the study of patterns. It's easy to be inspired by patterns as they are beautiful and unique and are all around us, from nature to architecture to trends.

HOW DOES IT HELP YOU TEACH MATH AND SUPPORT MATH EDUCATORS?

I use it as a warm-up routine. It's the most impactful routine because students are writing equations based on how they see the pattern. It's an organic process because it stems naturally from what they observe. Two people can see the same pattern grow (or shrink) in different ways. This simple fact encourages creativity and perseverance to find another way to see the pattern. The student then writes an expression for each part of the pattern based on how it grows or how it stays constant.

WHAT ADVICE WOULD YOU GIVE TO A TEACHER USING VISUAL PATTERNS FOR THE FIRST TIME?

I'd encourage teachers to play with the patterns themselves. It's much easier to teach something that we truly enjoy and believe in its impact. Visual patterns are an incredible tool to help students sharpen their pattern-seeking skills and develop algebraic reasoning. I've put together a comprehensive online grassroots workshop, How to Use Visual Patterns, in which I share how you can facilitate it as a warm-up routine. It's for all levels of users.

WHAT FEEDBACK HAVE YOU RECEIVED ABOUT THE ROUTINE THAT STUCK WITH YOU? (FROM TEACHERS OR STUDENTS)

These are some of the tweets that I got from teachers:

Follow

@fawnpnguyen Thank you thank you thank you. For the first time, they derived the explicit formula...... understand the "why", the "how", and why it's NOT the "always". Ss rocked the visual patterns and stayed engaged for days... helping each other see. Can't wait to keep going!

11:19 AM - 21 Sep 2019

Introduced visualpatterns.org to my students last week. A student (who generally dislikes maths/thinks she can't do it) came in today talking about the website and the patterns she's been working on. Over the WEEKEND. 😍😍😍

9:35 PM · Nov 8, 2020 · Twitter for iPhone

WHICH ONE DOESN'T BELONG? #WODB

WODB is one of my favorite activation routines for every grade level I teach and also with my daughter at home. The routine is very popular among math educators. Students are presented with four choices and asked, "Which One Doesn't Belong?" The beauty of the task is that an argument can be made for each choice, so it hooks students into sharing and participating without the fear of being incorrect. Dr. Christopher Danielson, who developed the idea, wrote an amazing children's book where kids can explore shapes by analyzing which one doesn't belong.

When reading the book, for this particular example, my daughter and I had the following exchange:

Me: Which one doesn't belong?
Mariana: The pentagon, Tata
Me: Why?
Mariana: The other ones have six sides 🙄
Me: 😎

We started playing with this routine a lot at home. Truth be told, sometimes we were not exploring something mathematical per se, instead we were just playing and having some conversations. We started making our own *WODBs* using toys and things we found around the house. As she got more comfortable with the routine, I asked her to start coming up with a reason for each choice which sometimes she wasn't too happy about.

We once used Lego *Star Wars* characters and these were her reasons:

Upper left: Smaller than the others
Upper right: Different color hands (the right hand is black)
Lower left: Not holding anything
Lower right: Wearing a mask

On a different occasion we got to discuss "one" using multiple representations for it through *WODB*. Playing with this routine has helped my daughter look at situations with different lenses. I also have enjoyed all the conversations we had where I get to see how she's thinking and making sense of the question.

The *WODB* site is nicely organized. There are three categories: shapes, numbers, and graphs. There are so many useful resources in there for anyone who is teaching or learning mathematics.

My experience with the routine with high schoolers hasn't been much different than my experience with my daughter. My students also love *WODB*. We probably have used most (if not all) of the examples on the website, so we had to start coming up with our own. Next is an example of a *WODB* I put together for my precalculus students to review some trigonometry.

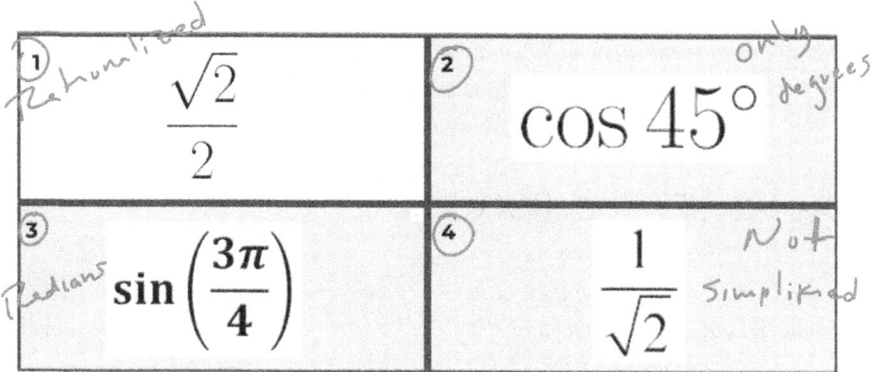

Using *WODB* to start class was a very effective way for the students who were at home to interact with the students that were in school when we were using a hybrid model (half of the students remote and half of the students in person). The students had so much to share and were so eager to do so that despite the challenging conditions. It really felt like the entire class came together.

If you want to learn more about the rationale and origins of *WODB*, I strongly suggest you visit Dr. Danielson's website talkingmathwithkids.com. There are many amazing resources and projects for anyone interested in learning or discussing mathematics. Back in 2015, Dr. Danielson wrote a short blog post titled, Building a Better Shapes Book (Which One Doesn't Belong).

Here is an excerpt from the blog you may find useful when learning about *WODB*:

There are many shapes books available for reading with children. Most of them are very bad. I have complained about this for years. Now I have done something about it. Most shapes books—whether board books for babies and toddlers, or more sophisticated books for school-aged children—are full of misinformation and missed opportunities. As an example, there is nearly always one page for squares and a separate one for rectangles. There is almost never a square on the rectangles page. That's a missed opportunity. Often, the text says that a rectangle has two short sides and two long sides. That's misinformation. A square is a special rectangle, just as a child is a special person. After years of contemplation, I had a kernel of an idea the other night. The kids are back in school before I am, so I had some flex time available. One thing led to another and voilá. A better shapes book.

HOW TO USE THIS BOOK

On every page are four shapes. The question is the same throughout the book—which one doesn't belong? For example, which shape doesn't belong in this set? If you are thinking, "It depends on how you look at it," then you've got the idea.

- *The bottom left shape doesn't belong because it's not shaded in.*
- *The top left shape doesn't belong because it only has three sides, while the others have four.*
- *The top right doesn't belong because it is the only square.*
- *The bottom right doesn't belong because it's the only one resting on a side.*

Maybe you have different reasons for some of these. That's great! The only measure of being right is whether your reason is true. With an infant, you can use this book like any other shapes book. Look at each page together. Point at each shape and talk about it as you snuggle. With a young child, ask which one doesn't belong and why. Most pages in the book have at least one shape that a young child can identify as not belonging. Join the conversation by pointing out a different shape that doesn't belong for some other reason. With an older child, challenge yourselves to find a reason for each of the 44 shapes in the book. There is no answer key. This is intentional–to encourage further discussion and to encourage you to return to the book to try again.

If you haven't done so already, I really hope you give *WODB* a chance with your students or your own children at home.

REFLECTION QUESTIONS

1. How do you normally start class? What are your students doing in the first 5-10 minutes of class?
2. What is your favorite activation routine to use with your students? Why is it your favorite?
3. What activation would you like to explore or learn more about? What benefits would it have for you and/or your students?

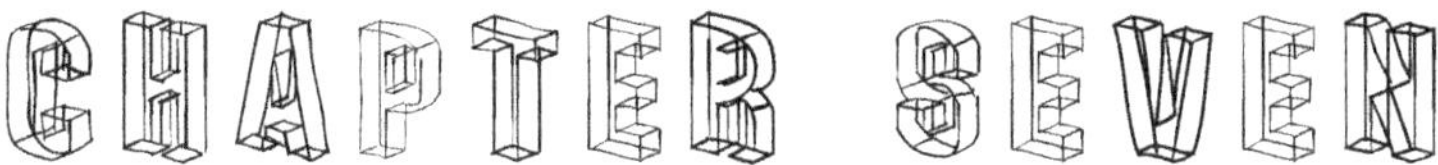

CHAPTER SEVEN

MATHEMATICS REVEALS ITS SECRETS ONLY TO THOSE WHO APPROACH IT WITH PURE LOVE, FOR ITS OWN BEAUTY.

ARCHIMEDES

WHAT DID I LEARN FROM FACILITATING MATHPLAY WITH MY STUDENTS?

FACILITATING MATHPLAY WITH MY students during the past few years has really transformed the way I teach. My main goal when I started doing it was for my students to enjoy learning mathematics the same way my daughter was enjoying it at home. Nowadays, whenever I'm planning a future lesson or unit, I'm always thinking about how I can incorporate more MathPlay into teaching and learning. I have learned and grown so much as an educator and discovered that a GCF (Greatest Common Factor) exists while facilitating MathPlay.

ENGAGEMENT

In general, anything involving "play" requires active participation from the players. MathPlay is no different. It requires students to actively explore or apply mathematical concepts and ideas. When I started facilitating MathPlay at home, I particularly enjoyed watching her think and try to make sense of whatever task we were exploring. There wasn't a specific set of instructions to follow, which she is very comfortable with. She had to think about the what and how of the problem. For example, to have my daughter practice her addition with carrying, I would give her a set of ten questions to complete. She would complete all ten but while she is doing that task, she's thinking about what she would do afterwards. How do I know? She would ask me something like, "Tata, when I finish can I watch the Powerpuff Girls?" She was compliant. Most of the time she would get all of the questions correct but it didn't mean she was fully engaged. However, when we were trying to recreate a two-dimensional shape in three dimensions using blocks she was thinking about what she had to do and how she could do it. When she was enjoying MathPlay, she wasn't given an algorithm to complete the task. Thinking about the "how" required her to be fully engaged.

With my high school students, I observed something very similar. Oftentimes, they wanted me to tell them exactly what to do so they could follow the directions and just do the work. For example, if I asked them what the equation of a circle centered at (2, -3) with radius 4 was, they would have no problem saying $(x-2)^2+(y+3)^2=16$. However, when their task was to recreate a picture from a movie using conic sections, they had to think more deeply about the task. They had to be fully engaged in figuring out "how" exactly to do that. I learned that having students think about the "how" can result in higher levels of engagement.

When facilitating MathPlay, you should also be able to hear it. If you walked by my classroom as students are working, you would probably hear a lot of noise. In my experience, when students are fully engaged your classroom is going to be louder than normal. There will be multiple questions, conversations, troubleshooting, and collaboration happening all around. When my students completed the Pringles circle activity for example, the room probably may have seemed a little chaotic to anyone walking by. Students were working in different groups; they needed their computers or cell phones to take pictures and be able to upload them. It may have seemed like they were doing different things, but they were all engaged in the task at hand. During my first years of teaching, I perceived a loud classroom as a classroom in need of better classroom management which I have learned is not always the case.

It's hard as a teacher not to jump in when students need or request help. However, allowing them to think and figure out things on their own is something that they also need to learn. Facilitating MathPlay can help fully engage students in their learning. Whether students are trying to figure out the "how" or they are just enjoying the task, MathPlay can be a useful strategy to engage students.

DEEPER UNDERSTANDING

As a teacher, I feel we are always time poor. Many times, I wish I had a little more time to show my students a different example, application, video, or activity to help them deepen their understanding. Teachers may be less likely to facilitate MathPlay if they perceive it as an "extra" activity just in case they have "extra" time. Since MathPlay can lead to higher levels of engagement, as a result, students can also achieve deeper levels of understanding. Personally, I feel that sometimes we teach mathematics too linearly. First, we do A, then we do B, and now that they know (or have seen) A and B, hopefully students will figure out C. I'm not criticizing this method as I use it in my classroom and there is a lot of value in providing scaffolds along the way for our students. However, sometimes I like to drop my students at step C. Just give them a task and let them figure out how to get there, let them figure out **their** steps A and B.

When my geometry students were learning about right triangles for example, they took pictures of triangles that looked like right triangles and their task was to prove that they were or weren't actually right triangles using *GeoGebra*. They were not given specific instructions on how to do so, the "how" was something they needed to determine. Students ended up using different approaches. Some students measured the sides of the triangle and used the Pythagorean theorem. Others found the slopes of the line segments to determine if the slopes were negative reciprocals, hence there would be a right angle. And some measured the interior angles of the triangle.

I could have done one or multiple examples where I went over all the different methods, however, it was so much more powerful for my students to discover the methods themselves. They were able to make connections within other math concepts like slope, which they had learned the previous year in algebra. They also got to practice their problem-solving skills when they had to figure out how to approach the problem. Most of the time when students approach a problem, they already have a set of steps to follow. MathPlay can be a tool to have students deepen their understanding by making connections and figuring out how to approach a problem.

Making connections in mathematics is so important. As a teacher, I wholeheartedly believe that we should make an effort to teach most (if not all) the different math classes our schools offer. I have had the opportunity to teach algebra, geometry, algebra 2, trigonometry, precalculus, and calculus. When you have experienced the "sequence" your students will follow, it gives you a better understanding of what they are coming in with and what they need for the next level. It gives you a deeper understanding of your students and the math they are learning. I'm not encouraging you to teach all new classes every year but expanding your experience will benefit you and your students. The same can be said for my elementary school colleagues. Teaching kindergarten will benefit first grade teachers as they have an understanding of where their students are coming from. Similarly, teaching second grade benefits the first grade teacher as well in that they have knowledge and understanding about where their students are going.

MORE THAN REQUIRED

As an eighth grader back in Colombia, I learned algebra from an awesome teacher, Mr. Quintero, who used the book *Algebra de Baldor*, a very popular book for teaching algebra in many Spanish speaking countries in Latin America. I remember at the end of every unit, there would be hundreds of practice problems. I was not required to do any of those, but I would do them to better prepare for the test. At the time, I felt that if I did every problem, then there was no way Mr. Quintero would be able to surprise me. Truth be told, I also needed good grades to keep my scholarship in the school. Doing more than you have to do requires intrinsic motivation. I felt prepared for every test I took in that class as I felt there were no other problems I could have done.

Intrinsic motivation is going to look different for every student and not every student is motivated by good grades. Don't get me wrong, if a student is not motivated by grades it does not imply they don't care about learning. We, as educators, should always make an effort to set a stage where students will be motivated to learn and be successful. When my daughter was learning how to count money, we went over all the different coin values and completed a few worksheets she was given in school. Then we started using a *GeoGebra* applet where she would use coins to make purchases of items with different prices. She had to figure out what coins to use and then "pay" at the register. She wanted to play this game forever. She bought every item then started using different combinations to buy it again. Her motivation, I believe, was that she wanted to play, a very natural desire for a seven-year-old.

At the end of the school year, it is now guaranteed that my precalculus students will complete a final *Desmos* art project where they can use all the different functions they learned during the school year. They choose an image they want to recreate using their knowledge and skills. When I first gave this project, I never imagined that there will be students who will write over one hundred equations involving different functions: linear, quadratic, cubic, trigonometric, rational, radical, etc, as well as different domain and range restrictions. The number of equations they had to use was not even mentioned in the instructions. I mentioned they should use at least eight different types of functions. However, students did so much more than they were required to do. I was so proud of them when we got to share some of their work in a blog for MAA. Read the full article by scanning the QR code.

Parents even shared that their children had worked so hard on the project and that they were so proud of their work. When I asked some students why they had written so many equations, I got responses like "Phineas is my all-time favorite character so I wanted the project to be perfect Mr. V." MathPlay can definitely lead to students doing more than required because they are truly enjoying what they are doing and learning.

OWNERSHIP

While enjoying MathPlay in our basement, Mariana would go off on a tangent to create her own pattern using geometric shapes or even to create her own "new" shape (that no one else knew). Whenever this happened, I could tell she felt empowered by math. She wasn't afraid to make a mistake as this was her very own creation. When she finished, I would ask her questions about the shape or the pattern in general. We would look for shapes inside the shape which always led to more and more fun MathPlay conversations.

My daughter felt empowered to use the math she was learning (or already knew) to create something of her own. The math she was learning became useful and fun in the world of a young elementary school student. During your time as an educator, how many times have you heard "When am I going to use this (insert math concept) in real life?" We can make this question something of the past. I'm the first one to admit that as the math concepts get more complex it may also be more challenging to find real world applications. However, we must also admit that it's not impossible, especially with today's technology and access to information.

For my daughter, learning math is not only a fun activity but also something she can use and apply in her life. We can extrapolate this idea throughout K-12. Math should be perceived as a fun language that can help us think more logically and make sense of the world around us. A step in that direction would involve giving students more ownership over their learning. At the secondary level, I have tried to do this in two different ways. One is by giving students some level of choice in how to demonstrate mastery of their knowledge. For example, instead of giving a traditional assessment like a quiz or test, allowing them to complete an alternative assignment like an art project or making a video explanation of a particular problem or task. Truth be told, this is not always an option but from time to time I try to make it an alternative for students that want to do it. I personally don't feel that an alternative assessment is necessarily less rigorous. I wouldn't be able to give a test where students have to write over one hundred equations, but they can choose to do it within their own project.

The second strategy I have used is giving students alternative assignments for independent or group practice. For example, instead of having the whole class complete the same set of problems on polygons. Every student walks around school (or their home), finds a real polygon and then analyzes all of its properties in depth. I know there is a downside to this model because students are not practicing every polygon. However, I have observed that their work becomes more meaningful when students choose what polygon to study. Facilitating MathPlay by providing more student choice can help students develop a sense of ownership over the mathematics they are learning, making their overall experience more meaningful.

COMMUNITY BUILDING

One of the most powerful lessons for me with MathPlay did not involve any mathematical content. During the past few years, I'm happy to share that my classroom has become a place where students build more than their mathematical skills. While we learned and grew together, we became a community in a way united by MathPlay. Because of the nature of MathPlay students were always naturally inclined to work with one another. It was almost necessary to activate each other as a learning resource since on many occasions there were no specific instructions on how to approach the task at hand. Also, there was only one Mr. Valencia who circulated around the classroom. So instead of waiting for me to arrive, students counted on each other for support.

I can't tell you how many times we were using a tech platform and students were trying to figure out something I did not know how to do myself. For example, how to color (shade in) their pictures in their art projects. They had all the different shapes, but we were not sure how to color them in. While I was thinking, a student suggested, "What if we use inequalities instead of equations?" It may seem like the obvious thing to do now but it was so powerful in that moment that the idea came from a student and not from myself. Students felt empowered to share their ideas and to support one another. As an aside, I also think there is a lot of value in students seeing that the teacher does not have all the answers at all times. Over time, I realized that with MathPlay we were fostering a community of math learners.

As students worked together in figuring out the task, more and more a team approach started to happen. There is something special that happens when a group of people accomplish something together. This is true not only in education. There is a sense of friendship that developed as students worked together towards a common goal. This is something that I wouldn't be able to quantify but there was a very positive atmosphere in the classroom. Think of the feeling you get with that class you REALLY enjoy teaching because you feel a special connection with your students. That special connection is mutual and creates a special synergy in the classroom that is very conducive to learning.

I really hope that we all get to build more communities of learners in our math classes. Math class can definitely be the class where students come to share and learn together. I believe that MathPlay can be a very useful tool in fostering communities in our classrooms. I'm not making an argument that if you facilitate MathPlay all your students will be happy and will enjoy math, but I firmly believe it would be a step in the right direction. As a teacher of high school juniors, I get to write many college recommendation letters. I usually have students complete a form with general information that would help me write their letter. In almost every form I read, students always mention at least one MathPlay activity they remember and how it made them feel at the time. I think it's time we create more happy memories in math class by facilitating more MathPlay.

CONNECTING BEYOND THE CONTENT

Many times, while students were enjoying MathPlay, they had to make decisions. What polygon to explore? What image to recreate? How to approach the problem? I believe they were empowered by this and I learned that the math conversations did not stop when math class was over. Colleagues from other departments shared that some of my students were discussing strategies and each other's art projects in their classes. A student who recreated a book cover she was reading in English, shared her project with her teacher. Other students shared their *Encanto* projects with their Spanish class while watching the movie. Some of the projects were posted on the school website's main page. I can tell you my students were really proud of their work and they were happy they got to share it beyond the four walls of our classroom.

I loved that they were able to see and apply math beyond our class. Math was not an abstract subject they would only talk about with Mr. Valencia. For the past few years, I have been teaching multiple sessions of precalculus. Most of the students are juniors who are enrolled in many of the same classes and sometimes they are taking the exact same classes at different times of the day. I learned that it was common for students from different sessions to get together on their own time to work on their math. Math was a reason to get together with a friend from a different class. A parent once reached out to me via Canvas (our LMS) to share that their son and son's friend were working on a project the whole day on a Saturday. The parent had asked them how it was going and their reply was that no specific length was required but they wanted it to be "perfect."

While facilitating MathPlay I learned that the math concepts students were learning became relevant in their lives. This wasn't necessarily because they were using logic rules and derivatives on a daily basis, but because they felt connected to what they were learning. There were students who shared about the math they were learning on their social media. I don't think there is stronger proof that something is relevant to a teenager than sharing about it on their social media platforms. They shared some of their math art self-portraits. Other students decided to make TikTok videos to explain a problem instead of submitting it in writing. As someone who loves and enjoys math, it makes me very happy to see this type of special connection between students and the math they are learning.

REFLECTION QUESTIONS

1. When are your students most engaged? How do you know?
2. How do you connect with your students beyond the content you teach?
3. Thinking of the classes you are currently teaching, are there opportunities to collaborate in cross-curricular topics?

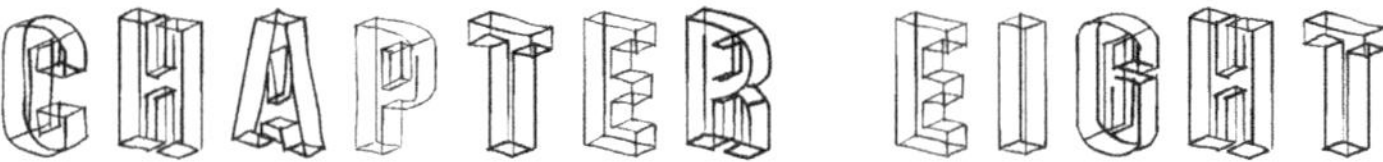

CHAPTER EIGHT

MATHEMATICS IS THE LANGUAGE WITH WHICH GOD HAS WRITTEN THE UNIVERSE.

GALILEO GALILEI

FULL DISCLOSURE

ONE OF THE GOALS in writing the book you're holding was to share my story and hopefully inspire you to facilitate more MathPlay with your students. With that in mind, I want to present the full picture of my MathPlay journey. As a classroom teacher, I don't think "One-Size Fits All" is a model we should be using with our students. This also applies to facilitating MathPlay, you, as the classroom teacher, know what will work best for your students and when. I wish I had an algorithm for how to facilitate MathPlay in every classroom but that's not realistic as our students are not machines we get to program. The success of MathPlay depends in part in how well we're able to connect with our students. I'd like to share some true facts about MathPlay from the perspective of a classroom teacher.

WHAT EXACTLY IS MATHPLAY?

For me, MathPlay is the combination of teaching and learning mathematics while bringing joy to my students. It is not exclusive for a particular age group or level. Anyone learning mathematics can enjoy MathPlay. It also does not depend on specific tools or technology. You can use anything that will make your students' experience more enjoyable and memorable. MathPlay is a strategy that will help you connect with your students while building a community of learners in your classroom. Finally, my definition of MathPlay is personal and shaped by my experiences with students. How would you define MathPlay?

NOT EVERYDAY

Facilitating MathPlay is not something that I'm able to do every day with my students or even with my daughter at home. I wish I was able to teach every lesson through MathPlay but I'm not there yet. Many times, with my daughter, we do mini lessons on topics she is learning, needs to review, or will be learning in the future. For example, before she has an assessment, we practice at home using our little whiteboards. At that point, I believe that is what she needs. We still do a lot of MathPlay on a regular basis but sometimes I feel that a more traditional approach might better serve her.

As an educator, I strive to improve my lessons from the previous year to the next. Even when I'm teaching the same class, two consecutive years, I try to improve different aspects of my lessons. As a result, I have lessons that I really like as I have found them to be very engaging and effective for students. Some of these lessons may not have a MathPlay component to it but that's ok, they're still good lessons. Just like my daughter, sometimes my students may also need to practice a very specific skill. So, we may use a platform for online formative assessment, like *Delta Math*, because that is what they need at that point. As teachers, we know what is best for our students.

If you have a great lesson for a particular topic, you don't have to make any changes to it. There may be other opportunities where you can incorporate MathPlay to engage your students in a different way. My point is that good teaching is good teaching, MathPlay is only a strategy that you, as the teacher, will determine when it would be most helpful or appropriate for your students. I particularly enjoy using it at the beginning of our units when we are just getting to explore the topic. In a way, the less they know about the topic the better.

In the last few years, I have been teaching multiple sessions of the same class. As a result, there have been times where I've gotten to facilitate the same MathPlay lesson with different classes on the same day. As you may expect, it never goes the same. I learned that classes of the same grade level tend to engage faster than classes of mixed grades which makes sense. Students within the same grade level may be more comfortable and friendly with one another. I'm not discouraging you from trying to facilitate MathPlay with mixed grade classes but understand it may take longer for students to be comfortable with one another.

Another very important thing to consider is that if something is happening outside of school, or in the world in general, this may have an impact on students' willingness to play. Sadly, anytime you watch the news lately, it feels like something terrible is taking place somewhere. Of course, this is something out of our hands but it's something we need to keep in mind as we develop or present our lessons.

NOT EVERY TOPIC

While facilitating MathPlay with my students, I have learned that there are topics across different classes where MathPlay ideas just naturally flow for me. As you can imagine, there are also topics for which I'm still trying to figure out how to incorporate MathPlay. I honestly don't think the ability to facilitate MathPlay depends on the class or the topic itself. I believe that our experience, comfort level with the topic, and personal interests are what really makes the difference. If you asked me to facilitate MathPlay in AP Computer Science I would probably find it challenging as I haven't had the opportunity to teach that class yet. Does that imply that it can't be done? Or that other teachers will also have a hard time? Absolutely not. So, what do we need? We need each other. The more we are able to learn from one another, the more we and our students will grow and benefit. Every time I experience some level of success facilitating MathPlay with my students or my daughter, I love to share about the activity via Twitter as I wholeheartedly believe that knowledge is meant to be shared. I'm not claiming by any means that what I share will always work for every teacher in every context. My hope is that it will work for some and hopefully will inspire others.

Teaching experience and content knowledge can definitely impact one's ability to facilitate MathPlay. Feeling comfortable with a particular topic and having taught it before does give you a different lens. However, personal interests may also play an important role. If you are teaching a topic that you can relate to something you or your students enjoy, this may be a fantastic opportunity for MathPlay.

Recently, I was teaching a geometry class and students were learning about two column proofs. In my experience, this is a topic that not all students seem to enjoy. I wanted to review for the upcoming assessment, but I wanted students to work together completing the proof in a different way. Rather than having each student write out the proof, students were given little rectangular pieces of paper with all the statements and reasons. Their task was then to organize the proof, which required collaboration and a different approach. I knew many students in this particular class enjoyed building and solving puzzles. The students were highly engaged solving the "puzzle" proofs and it was an awesome way to review.

If you want to facilitate MathPlay in a topic or unit but aren't sure how, there are two things I would recommend. First, reach out to a colleague who's teaching (or has taught) the same class. The teacher next door may already have an idea that worked well for students or may be able to provide a different approach. Second, I always get ideas from educators on Twitter. I have also reached out to people both inside and outside the US with questions I think they may be able to help me with based on what they share. I must say that my experience has been very positive and have discovered that most educators on Twitter are willing to help and share.

DOES NOT ALWAYS REQUIRE TECHNOLOGY BUT IT CAN HELP

After teaching for fourteen years in three different school districts and three different colleges, I feel that one of the biggest deterrents preventing educators from trying new things is their comfort level with the technology it may involve. Facilitating MathPlay does not always involve technology. There are tech tools that can help (discussed in Chapter 5) but it's not a requirement. Teachers within the same department may have very different comfort levels with technology which is completely understandable. Nowadays, I feel comfortable using different technologies in my classroom as I have experienced different tools with my students. That being said, I still worry about the what ifs. What if it doesn't work? What if it crashes? What if someone comes in to observe while the technology fails?

Regardless of your comfort level with technology these are all valid questions for any teacher. Many times, when I'm able to help a colleague with a tech issue, I'm able to do so because at some point I had the exact same problem. The more you embrace tech tools, the more comfortable you will feel with them. I would venture to say that the vast majority of our students are very comfortable using technology. I can't tell you how many times my students have helped me troubleshoot a tech issue before, during, or after a lesson. I feel very comfortable asking my students for help and their response has always been very positive. When I'm facilitating a MathPlay lesson that relies on technology, here are some of the things I do that help me feel more comfortable:

I always try out whatever I'm using with students myself to make sure it works. I may even ask a colleague to play student. I also have an alternative plan which can be a PDF or print out version of the lesson. It may even be a different lesson or the next day's lesson. I have also invited administrators to my room, sharing that I would be trying something new and I'd love for them to stop by if they are available. I'm not suggesting that you should do exactly as I have done. I only want to share some ideas that have worked for me. If you want to facilitate MathPlay to engage your students, it will show. Your students will know you're trying to do something for them, and they will support you.

As a teacher, I'm the first to admit that I like to have control of my classes. I'm not referring to students or their behavior but more to the lesson itself. Not knowing if the technology is going to work can be challenging but that shouldn't be the reason we do not try new things. If we want our students to have a growth mindset, we should model it for them. We may use MathPlay as a strategy or technology as a tool, however, our lessons must always be centered around our students.

START SMALL

I think that the best advice for someone who is going to start MathPlay is to start small. Your first activity shouldn't be a major project that relies heavily on tech tools, for example. Instead, it may involve a small portion of your lesson; maybe within your activation at the beginning or consolidation at the end. Just to get students used to the idea of MathPlay in class, which they may also be experiencing for the very first time. It's important that we not attach any grades to MathPlay activities, at least in the beginning. We must allow students to MathPlay with the intention of exploring rather than assessing.

Once your students are familiar with the idea of MathPlay, it is time to move to the next level: building a full lesson around MathPlay. If you are concerned about it and want to be safe, maybe this could be a review day before an assessment. Have students apply what they already know in a less traditional context. Students will feel more comfortable with the idea of MathPlay and it will naturally grow for the class. By not attaching grades to the activity, students will feel safer to make mistakes without any repercussions.

As you complete more MathPlay lessons with your students, you will start to notice what works best for them. However, I strongly encourage you to specifically ask your students for feedback. My students have provided transformational feedback that has helped me become a better teacher for them. I used to think that asking students for feedback would be perceived as a deficiency, as though I didn't know what I was doing but this is far from accurate. I usually start by sharing that this is a new approach I think we can enjoy and that I'd love to hear their feedback so we can make it work better. I also asked students to share however they are more comfortable. Some students will be comfortable voicing their opinions in front of the class, but others won't. I try to give students some alternatives in how they can share. Sometimes I add an anonymous slide at the end of the lesson where they can share feedback. I invite students to send me an email, or have a conversation with me after class. I also recommend asking students to tell me specifics so we can work together to make our activities engaging for all learners.

If your first MathPlay lessons involve a big project that is graded, this will definitely create some anxiety for you and your students. It's likely students will prioritize their grade over an opportunity to play, so start small. If a MathPlay lesson does not go as planned, please don't be discouraged. Think of your rationale behind it. Why are you facilitating MathPlay? I want them to naturally explore and be able to apply what they are learning in different contexts. So even if a lesson does not go as planned, I will still try it because I wholeheartedly believe it can be a powerful strategy for my students to experience.

REFLECTION QUESTIONS

1. What do you normally do when a lesson does not go as planned?
2. How do you motivate students to learn without worrying about grades?
3. What is your reason for wanting to facilitate MathPlay?

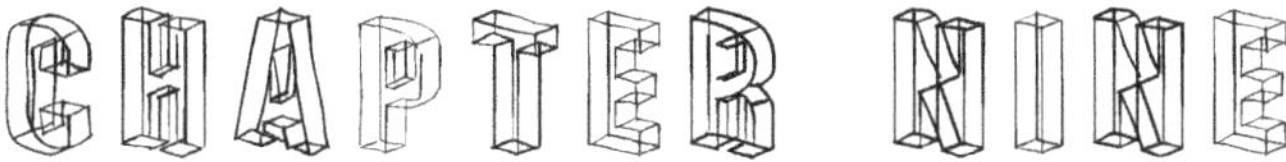

IT'S NOT TRUE THAT PEOPLE STOP PURSUING DREAMS BECAUSE THEY GROW OLD, THEY GROW OLD BECAUSE THEY STOP PURSUING THEIR DREAMS.

GABRIEL GARCIA MARQUEZ

WHAT COMES NEXT?

I WOULD LIKE TO continue MathPlay at home with my daughters and in school with my students. My older daughter is going into second grade so there will be new concepts for us to explore. She's already comfortable with MathPlay and I hope to continue to integrate math to her daily life. My younger daughter has also started to enjoy MathPlay by identifying numbers and counting up to ten. Like most younger siblings, Madeline wants to do whatever her older sister does, so when Mariana and I are playing, she sits next to us pretending alongside. I'm very excited to try the MathPlay activities we developed with my little one, I'm sure she will give the activities a different spin. I'm also excited to create more MathPlay activities for her based on the things she likes.

With my high school students, I also plan to continue to facilitate more MathPlay. As classroom teachers, we don't have full control over what classes we get to teach, but regardless of the class I would like to create more MathPlay activities and improve the ones I already have. Currently, I have at least one MathPlay activity per unit of study within the classes I have taught in the last three years. My plan is to grow the collection to at least two per unit of study if I'm teaching the same class or start a collection for a new class. I think that by now, many students coming into my class know beforehand that there will be MathPlay, which is awesome. They know because of friends that had me or they have seen some of the projects that are shared via social media through school channels. Wouldn't it be amazing if all of our learners expected math class to be fun and engaging? Wouldn't it help change the negative perception of mathematics in society?

I know that the idea of MathPlay will continue to grow and expand with my daughters and my students as there is still so much work to be done. Something I'd like to try is including my daughters or my students in the development of MathPlay ideas. To this point, I have developed the ideas based on what they are learning while trying to incorporate things that I think they would like or enjoy. If students are provided with a structure, they will be able to create their own MathPlay activities. This may be something that will be easier for older students because they are more independent. After experiencing MathPlay in a few units, I would like to give students the opportunity to create a MathPlay activity for any lesson within the unit. I'd have to think more about it, but I know that our students' creativity has no boundaries.

In my experience facilitating MathPlay, I've learned that technology can be very useful and appealing for our learners. Whether they are at the elementary or secondary level, students are very comfortable embracing technology in their learning. I feel that I'm somewhat comfortable using different tech tools in the classroom, but I acknowledge it takes time to fully learn them. In this book I mentioned four tools: Graspable Math, Desmos, GeoGebra, and the Math Learning Center. The truth is that I'm still learning about these tools. I don't think there will be a time when I feel I know everything about any of these programs. I feel I know enough about them to engage my students in the context of our lessons. If I waited until I knew everything about the tool or platform, then it's very likely I wouldn't use it in class.

There are other tech tools and platforms I'm currently learning and exploring like: *Mathigon, Autograph, SAM Labs, ChatGPT,* and *Math Whiteboard* just to name a few. My goal is to have more options for MathPlay with my students and my daughters at home. I know it can be overwhelming to decide which tool to learn or use in the classroom as there are so many out there that promise to be "game changers." Something I always try to do before exploring a tool is hearing from another educator who has used it. I often ask people via Twitter and get pretty on point feedback. I also try to think critically about the time it will take to learn and implement the tool versus the benefits for my students. Just because there is a "game changer" tool out there, does not mean it will be a good fit for you or your students.

I really hope that what I have shared in this book will inspire educators to facilitate more MathPlay in their classroom with their students. I absolutely love when teachers share about an idea and how it went. Not too long ago, a teacher from Australia shared about their Pringles Ringle challenge. We exchanged some messages via Twitter and I had shared some ideas. He commented, "This looks fun. I'll give it a try." I was so happy when he shared what his students had done. I also learned that Pringles in Australia look different from Pringles in the United States. They're flatter. But you can still make a circle!

One of my goals is to continue to share what MathPlay is all about so that more people are inspired to try it. I would eventually love to start a PLC of educators who are facilitating MathPlay in their classrooms. Sharing ideas and talking about what works and what hasn't will allow us to grow in our practice. We are definitely better together and our impact on students will be exponential. With today's technology, we have the ability to collaborate far beyond our school walls. We will not only be making math class more fun and engaging but we'll be contributing to changing society's negative perception of mathematics. What better time than now to make math class every student's favorite? And what better way to start than with MathPlay?

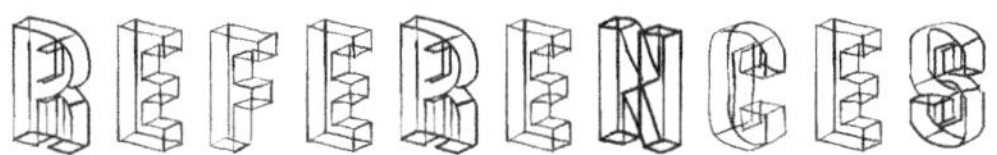

REFERENCES

INTRODUCTION

Facts about Teaching: Respect Project, National Conversations … - Ed. https://www2.ed.gov/documents/respect/teaching-profession-facts.doc.

CHAPTER 1

University of Cambridge. "Learning through 'guided' play can be as effective as adult-led instruction up to at least age eight: Play-based learning may also have a more positive effect on younger children's acquisition of important early maths skills compared with traditional, direct instruction." ScienceDaily. ScienceDaily, 12 January 2022. <www.sciencedaily.com/releases/2022/01/220112094006.htm>

CHAPTER 3

"The Pringle Ringle." Questioning My Metacognition, 20 Jan. 2019, https://gfletchy.com/the-pringle-ringle/

Peter Liljedahl, https://www.peterliljedahl.com/

"Open Middle®." Open Middle®, 21 Oct. 2020, https://www.openmiddle.com/

CHAPTER 4

/u/daniel+Mentrard. "Polar Coordinates in Battleship." GeoGebra, 5 Feb. 2020, https://www.geogebra.org/m/gzzp5whu

/u/pantaloni. "Optimisation Du Volume D'une Boîte." GeoGebra, https://www.geogebra.org/m/g3faZP2A

Trigonometric Ratios: Ahsoka Tano
https://www.reddit.com/r/PrequelMemes/comments/j65v8a/wanted_to_repost_my_favorite_star_wars_meme_ive/

CHAPTER 5

"Bridges in Mathematics: The Math Learning Center: MLC." Bridges in Mathematics | The Math Learning Center | MLC, https://www.mathlearningcenter.org/

"Graspable Math Activities." Graspable Math Activities, https://activities.graspablemath.com/

"Let's Learn Together." Desmos, https://www.desmos.com/

"The World's Favorite, Free Math Tools Used by over 100 Million Students and Teachers." GeoGebra, https://www.geogebra.org/

CHAPTER 6

Howiehua.wordpress.com, https://howiehua.wordpress.com/

"Same but Different Math." SAME BUT DIFFERENT MATH, https://www.samebutdifferentmath.com/

"Visual Patterns." Visual Patterns, https://www.visualpatterns.org/

with special thanks to Christopher Danielson and his Which One Doesn't Belong - A Shapes Book., et al. "Which One Doesn't Belong?" Wodb.ca, https://wodb.ca/

Trianglemancsd. "Talking Math with Your Kids." Talking Math With Your Kids, https://talkingmathwithkids.com/

Trianglemancsd. "Which One Doesn't Belong? A Better Shapes Book." Talking Math With Your Kids, https://

talkingmathwithkids.com/shop/which-one-doesnt-belong-a-better-shapes-book/

Trianglemancsd. "Building a Better Shapes Book [Which One Doesn't Belong?]." Talking Math With Your Kids, https://talkingmathwithkids.com/news/building-a-better-shapes-book-2/

CHAPTER 7

Valencia, Libardo. "Maa Blog: Engaging Math Students with Art." MATH VALUES, MATH VALUES, 24 Nov. 2021, https://www.mathvalues.org/masterblog/engaging-students-with-a-desmos-art-project

IMAGES USED

Ahsoka Tano from *Star Wars* franchise, 2008, Disney+
Mirabel Madrigal from *Encanto*, 2021, Disney
Dolores Madrigal from *Encanto*, 2021, Disney

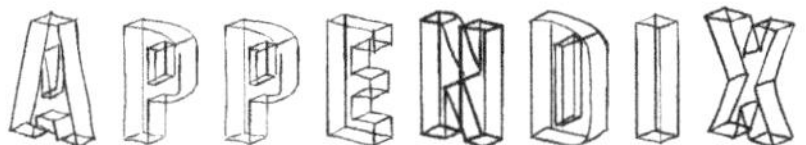

TINY POLKA DOT

Daniel Finkel

https://mathforlove.com/awg/tiny-polka-dot/

PATTERN BLOCKS AND BOARDS CLASSIC TOY

Melissa & Doug

https://www.melissaanddoug.com/products/pattern-blocks-and-boards-classic-toy

100 PIECE WOOD BLOCKS SET

Melissa & Doug

https://www.melissaanddoug.com/products/100-piece-wood-blocks-set

CREATED BY ME! BIRDHOUSE WOODEN CRAFT KIT

Melissa & Doug

https://www.melissaanddoug.com/products/created-by-me-birdhouse-wooden-craft-kit

DECONSTRUCTING GEOMETRY MAGNET SET

Public Math

https://www.public-math.org/support/geometrymagnets

ABOUT THE AUTHOR

Libo Valencia is a mathematics teacher at Horace Greeley High School in Chappaqua, NY. He is an adjunct lecturer at his alma mater, CUNY Lehman College and teaches at the Science and Technology Entry Program (STEP) at Mercy College. With fourteen years of experience, Libo is a passionate educator who strongly believes that understanding mathematics can help all students develop critical thinking and problem-solving skills that can be utilized beyond the classroom. Libo is known for his constant use of different technologies to engage his students by bringing math concepts to life. As a mathematics educator, Libo has taught a wide range of subjects, from remedial algebra classes to upper-level calculus. He is committed to helping spread the joy of mathematics through MathPlay. Libo wholeheartedly believes that facilitating MathPlay helps students develop a deeper appreciation for math and empowers them to better understand it. He has presented and facilitated workshops related to MathPlay and his professional experiences for educators in the United States and the United Kingdom. Libo holds a Bachelor of Arts in Mathematics, a Master of Arts in Pure Mathematics, and a Master of Science in Educational Leadership. Libo is happily married to his wife Carolina and has two beautiful daughters, Mariana and Madeline.

libardo.valencia33@gmail.com

@MrValencia24

@MrValencia24

libovalencia.com

CODE BREAKER INC.

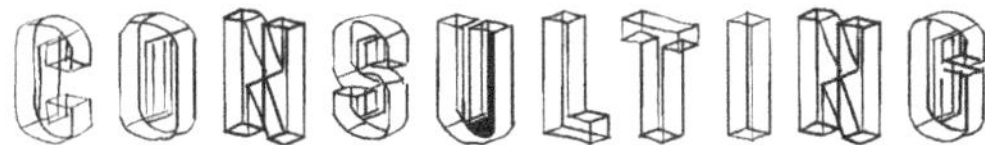

To learn more about

LIBO VALENCIA

or to book him for a visit to your school, district, or event, visit www.codebreakeredu.com

Code BREAKER

INSPIRE · INNOVATE

LEAD · TEACH · LEARN

CODE BREAKER LEADERSHIP SERIES

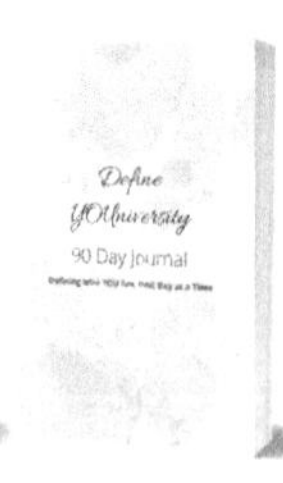

CODE BREAKER KID COLLECTION

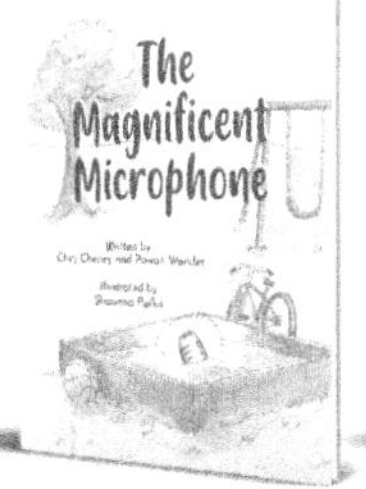

THE X FACTOR LIBRARY

Code
BREAKER
www.codebreakeredu.com

Made in United States
North Haven, CT
05 July 2023

38578326R00089